She
Knows Best

She Knows Best

Business Wisdom
from Extraordinary Women

PRESENTED BY MOLLEY RICKETTS

PAULA BARMORE | AMY RUDY | AMY SIMPSON

PAMELA FULTON BROADUS | LAUREN BROADUS | JENNA AHERN

Publishing support provided by
Ignite Press
55 Shaw Ave. Suite 204
Clovis, CA 93612
www.IgnitePress.us

ISBN: 979-8-9939238-0-2
ISBN: 979-8-9939238-1-9 (E-book)

For bulk purchases and for booking, contact:

Molley Ricketts
molley@incipioworks.com
incipioworks.com

Cover design by Muhammad Akram
Edited by Elizabeth Arterberry
Interior design by Jetlaunch

FIRST EDITION

• • •

The Authors

Molley Ricketts
Head Honcho

🌐 incipioworks.com

in linkedin.com/in/molleyricketts

f facebook.com/molley.ricketts

▶ https://www.youtube.com/@incipioworks

Paula D. Barmore
Real Estate Broker, Speaker, Community Builder

in linkedin.com/in/paula-barmore-a055005

f facebook.com/paula.barmore

📷 instagram.com/paulabarmore/

Amy Rudy

Sales and Growth Coach, Advisor, Speaker

🌐 impactsalessystems.com

in linkedin.com/in/amyrudy

Amy Simpson

Human Resources Consultant and Leadership Coach

🌐 www.soarconsultingllc.com

in linkedin.com/in/aesimpson

Pamela Fulton Broadus & Lauren Broadus

Pamela Fulton Broadus (President & CEO) &
Lauren Broadus (Chief Operations Officer)

splendideventsllc.org

facebook.com/SplendidEventsLLCKY

linkedin.com/in/pamela-fulton-broadus

linkedin.com/in/lauren-broadus

Jenna Ahern

CEO & Founder

guardianowldigital.com

app.guardianowlai.com

youtube.com/@Guardianowldigital

http://bit.ly/4nOnRBr

Table of Contents

Foreword by Maggie Harlow

D id you know there are records of male-owned businesses carved on Sumerian tablets from as far back as 3500 BCE?

Let's do the math. . .

Men: 5,500 years of experience owning businesses.
Women: 37 years of experience owning businesses.

It's breathtaking. Men have over 5,500 years of history, momentum, investment, and expertise in business cultivated primarily for themselves and their male heirs, friends, family, and colleagues.

Remember, in America, it was only **37 years ago, in 1988**, that a law was passed requiring a bank or credit company to extend a loan and credit to an eligible woman without requiring a male cosigner. Some women, in fact, resorted to having their very own sons cosign for them to start their businesses. What a load of shit!

How are things going?

In 1972, 4.6% of businesses were woman-owned.
In 2019, 42% of businesses were woman-owned.

And we have only just begun, sisters.

The essays and stories in this book, curated by Molley Ricketts, contain testimonies of women who are forging their financial freedom, discovering their potential, and now invite other women to put their shoulder to the wheel, calling them forward to their own destinies.

I started my own business in 2003. I didn't start my business because I wanted to build a fortune or break some kind of record. I wasn't seeking notoriety or dreaming of creating world-shaking innovations.

Like many women, I started a business because of frustration. I was working in an industry and a job I had no passion for. My bosses did not "see me" at my job—I felt invisible.

And I wanted my "ordinary day" to be something I was proud of and excited about.

I felt an undeniable call to explore what I'm capable of.

I've owned my Signarama sign franchise since 2003, and have launched and sold a few other businesses along the way. I raised a family, and my own husband came to work with me, enriching our relationship once we figured out how not to smother each other at our desks.

I have been profoundly successful, despite many setbacks and failures along the way. I have won many awards and been recognized as an involved citizen in our beautiful city.

My sons were only two and five years old when we started this business, so they watched me build this business from nothing to generating $5M in sales with over 30 employees.

One of my favorite stories about my kids involves the time when our franchise CEO came for a visit and stayed in our home. At one point, he asked my ten-year-old son, "Where is your mom's iron?"

My son said, unblinkingly, "She doesn't have one."

Confused, the franchise founder hoped to clarify his question by asking, "No, what does your mom *do*?"

"She works at Signarama." My son replied.

My son was right; I had thrown my iron away one day out of frustration, irked that I had been designated the unofficial ironing person in our home. I put an end to that, much to my delight and my franchise CEO's shock.

My husband and I raised our two sons to be independent and industrious. Our eldest son, Jack Harlow, threw off all societal norms and successfully pursued a career as a global rap star. His younger brother, Clay Harlow, inspired by this entire family of self-starters, became a music producer and works for himself, helping artists like his older brother, Jack.

My business has matured, along with me, to a point where the younger, more talented people working for me run it day-to-day. It is a wonderful place to be in life, to be asked to contribute a forward for this book and be able to eagerly say *"yes!"*

Reading this book absolutely thrills me.

What I love about the women who contributed to this beautiful book is how "real" they all are. I know them all. They love what they do as business owners, even though the work can be humiliating, difficult, messy, stressful, and crammed with failures big and small, which can make them want to fall to their knees out of exhaustion some days.

You won't find stories of easy success, attending glamorous client meetings in a dashing tailored suit, with clients throwing money across the table. This isn't about the "postable" moments, when we want to convince ourselves and our followers that "everything is good!"

Instead, you will find the grit, heartbreak, fear, and challenges that must be overcome to build something you love.

Why is this book important?

Every author in this book is a torchbearer, offering her generous spirit and her light for those navigating the dark and rocky path of entrepreneurship. Each holds her torch aloft for future women business owners or leaders who may be seeking warm and wise words.

They hold their torch for you, so please light your own and carry it along with you. Your torch will also offer light and inspiration to the daughters, sisters, nieces, mothers, aunts, and grannies who come along behind you.

Trust that, while the path of entrepreneurship may be treacherously difficult at times, your sisters are here to help. Seek out other women business owners to join you on your journey, as they are eager and deft collaborators.

No, this book isn't a stone tablet from Sumeria, but do not underestimate the power of great stories in making you feel like these writers are right beside you.

Introduction: When She Knows Best

There's a moment in every woman's story when she realizes she's been waiting for permission, clarity, the right time, someone else to say, "You're ready."

And then, something shifts. She stops waiting. She decides.

That's what this book is about.

When we began putting *She Knows Best* together, the goal wasn't to create another collection of success stories. It was to build a mirror, one reflecting the courage, grit, doubt, and grace that every woman carries on her way to becoming who she is meant to be. These stories are written by women who didn't wait to be chosen. They built. They led. They took risks. They rose.

Each chapter embodies a lived lesson on what it means to define yourself on your own terms:

- In "The Power of Connections," **Paula Barmore** reminds us that relationships are currency. They're not the transactional kind, but the soul-level kind that opens doors decades later. Her story celebrates community, service, and the magic that happens when women show up for one another.
- **Pamela and Lauren Broadus** take us behind the scenes of Splendid Events, LLC in "Making an Event Out of Life."

They show how entrepreneurship is both an act of faith and a family affair, providing a lesson in resilience, alignment, and purpose. Their partnership as mother and daughter is a testament to the fact that leadership and love can coexist and even thrive together.

- **Amy Rudy's** "She Closed the Gap—Between Her Ears" takes us into the one battlefield we all face: the one inside our own minds. She dismantles fear, self-doubt, and the limiting beliefs that whisper "you can't." Her chapter is a masterclass in mental toughness, reframing failure, and stepping into one's full, unfiltered confidence.

- **Amy Simpson's** "Charting Your Career Flight Path" gives every reader a compass. She identifies the barriers, assumptions, limiting beliefs, misinterpretations, and inner voices that hinder women's progress, and teaches us how to confront them directly. Her framework transforms fear into clarity and clarity into flight.

- **Jenna Ahern**, in "Permission Claimed, Not Granted," writes with raw honesty about what it means to build something from scratch without waiting for the green light. Her journey from Division 1 athlete to seven-figure CEO is more than a story of business growth. It's a declaration that no woman needs permission to lead boldly or reinvent herself when the world changes.

- Then there's "No One's Coming: So I Did." My story. The truth about starting Incipio Workforce Solutions from a messy desk and with a full heart. It's about the reality of leadership, building something that didn't exist yet, all while juggling motherhood, marriage, and the quiet ache of exhaustion. It's a story about refusing to shrink when the system says you should.

Together, these chapters create a mosaic of modern womanhood in modernity within the realm of business, not polished for perfection, but real, raw, and alive. This book is for the woman who's still waiting for the "right time." For the leader second-guessing her worth. For the mom, mentor, and maker who keeps showing up even when it's hard. It's for the dreamers who've learned that balance is possible, burnout is not a badge of honor, and bold solutions are born when women lead together.

You'll see yourself in these stories. Maybe not in the details, but in the heartbeat, the call to rise. Because "she knows best" isn't about having all the answers. It's about knowing when it's time to bet on yourself.

Take a deep breath, sister. Turn the page.

You already know what to do next.

CHAPTER 1

No One's Coming: So I Did

Molley Ricketts

Head Honcho

incipioworks.com

linkedin.com/in/molleyricketts

facebook.com/molley.ricketts

https://www.youtube.com/@incipioworks

As CEO of Incipio Workforce Solutions, Molley Ricketts leverages more than 25 years of experience with one guiding belief: when people thrive, businesses and communities thrive. Her mission is to help organizations reduce their greatest expense through long-term partnerships that bring innovation to recruitment, professional development, and retention.

Molley's expertise spans high-volume entry-level hiring to executive succession planning and strategic growth. Having worked with companies of all sizes, she understands the challenges and opportunities in building workforces that perform and stay engaged. With Incipio, she set out to help small and mid-sized companies rethink how they attract, retain, and support talent.

Over the past decade—and especially during the last four years—she and her team have emphasized the value of an engaged workforce as the foundation of organizational success. Today, Incipio partners with clients nationwide, with a strong focus on supporting essential workers in manufacturing, healthcare, and hospitality.

Beyond her professional life, Molley is dedicated to her community and cherishes time with family and friends, especially near the water. She and her husband and high school sweetheart, Chad, have two adult children and co-host *Lake Life with Molley and Chad*, a podcast now in its fourth season that celebrates lake living and connection.

• • •

A real-world playbook for leading with grit, building with heart, and staying true to your vision when the system says, "Shrink."

WHEN YOU KNOW, YOU KNOW (EVEN IF IT TERRIFIES YOU)

There wasn't a stage in my career when I didn't work late, after the kids went to bed, sneaking in time with top talent who couldn't talk during the day. That grind, that extra effort, was never acknowledged in my corporate role. Still, I kept going.

Balancing marriage, childcare, home, work, friendships, and even just breathing sat on my shoulders like extra shifts no one talked about. It didn't matter how carefully I planned, how efficiently I worked, or how loudly I screamed in frustration. The next day always showed up, and I had to show up with it.

I wasn't planning to start a company. I was just tired. Tired of watching companies hire wrong, lead wrong, and burn out the very people they claimed to care about. Tired of watching talented workers, especially women, be overlooked. Tired of watching essential workers be asked to do more with less. . . and attributing their hard work to leadership. It was happening everywhere I looked.

Then, one day, my husband Chad looked at me and said, "I don't understand why you keep going into companies to make them money when you could be doing this for yourself, for us. You could be building something bigger. Something better. Something that helps other women do the same."

That was it.

I started Incipio Workforce Solutions from a messy desk in the corner of my house. No investors. No manual. Just two decades of experience, a fire in my belly, and the unshakable belief that the workforce, my family and I, and my fellow women juggling everything deserved better.

That was over a decade ago. Since then, we've grown, pivoted, restructured, cried, celebrated, and stayed in the work. If you're expecting a story wrapped in a bow, this isn't it. This is the real version, the one I wish someone had handed me when I was wondering, *Can I really do this?*

THE REAL BEGINNING: LONGER DAYS, NIGHTS, AND THE LIE THAT SOMEONE'S COMING TO HELP

The early days of Incipio were built in the margins of a spare-bedroom-turned-office, then a makeshift setup in our basement. I didn't fully know what I was getting into, but I knew I was all in. The clients I had believed in the different approach to talent and engagement that Incipio offered. I've said it before and I'll say it again: when your work no longer reflects your worth, your values, or your voice, it's a sign. You don't need a justification to make a change that leads to personal and professional growth. We were made for more.

What I didn't realize, though, was how *isolating* this would feel. Here's the truth they don't print in entrepreneurship books: you're considered "unemployed" until you've got three years of *successful* business ownership under your belt. That means no banks, no investments, no traditional support to make your dream a reality. It's just you. And if you're a woman? Buckle up. It's worse.

Before we go any further, we need to name what so many of us have quietly navigated for years: the subtle (and not-so-subtle) misogyny that still shows up in the rooms in which we've worked hard to earn our place.

1974 was the year women were finally allowed to open credit cards in their own name, thanks to the Equal Credit Opportunity Act. Before that? Everything, from the bank account to the mortgage, was in "Mr. and Mrs." format, no matter how capable the "Mrs." was.

It wasn't that long ago, **1988** to be exact, that a woman needed a male relative to cosign a business loan. That's when the Women's Business Ownership Act finally passed. I once met a woman who helped push that legislation forward through NAWBO (National Association of Women Business Owners). She told us her 17-year-old *son* had to cosign her business loan because she didn't have a living husband, father, or brother.

> Unless you pee standing up, there are more hoops, more doubt, and more damn gatekeeping in building a business.

It still blows my mind that my mother's generation had to ask for permission to access their own financial resources. Even checking accounts weren't reliably available to women until the 1960s. So, yes, I know I was born at the *right* time. But the fact that it took *that* long still lights a fire in me. The truth most people don't want to say out loud is:

Unless you pee standing up, there are more hoops, more doubt, and more damn gatekeeping in building a business.

I didn't know any of this when I started. I had no idea how hard it would be to be taken seriously by financial institutions, or how long it would take to build enough credibility to earn their respect. They don't care about your vision. They want years' worth of tax returns and trailing numbers. And if you're a woman? They want a few extras.

Building a business is hard for anyone. But for women? It's an upriver voyage with a headwind. And we still do it anyway. Grit. Grind. Grace. That's the rhythm. That's the formula. Even with all that, the 3 a.m. wake-ups, selling a vision that others struggle to see while fighting my own doubts, and needing to learn to trust my voice while leading a team, I wouldn't trade it.

Entrepreneurship, for me, feels a lot like "The Beast" at Kings Island, a thrill ride park in southern Ohio known for pushing limits. The Beast is a legendary wooden roller coaster that snakes through dense forest with raw speed, brutal turns, underground tunnels, and two relentless lift hills. It hits 64 miles per hour and never lets up. Riding in the pitch black of night prevents you from seeing what's coming next, and that's exactly what makes it so unforgettable.

There are no shoulder straps. No harnesses. Just a single lap bar between you and the open air. It was literally designed to *throw you out* unless you hold on for dear life. That, in my mind's eye, *is* entrepreneurship: the excitement, the fear, and the full-body commitment it takes to build something that doesn't exist yet. . . and to hold on, white-knuckled, with everything you've got.

All of a sudden, almost without trying, you find yourself attracting this incredible wave of talent. People who *get it.* People who want to run alongside you and help bring the vision to life. And you realize, with deep humility, that you're not just building a business, you're building something worth sharing. Something that inspires others to leap, too. I found myself surrounded by powerhouse women founders, C-suite leaders, and business owners, and I leaned in, sometimes just to ask, *WTF do I do here?* The beautiful thing? Because I led with vulnerability, they showed up. Like a momma bird spreading her wings in the middle of a storm, they covered me. Sometimes just for a moment. Sometimes with a solution. Sometimes, they became the women who now stand beside me: strong, loyal, and fierce.

Red Rover, Red Rover, I dare you to come over. *Women.* I can hardly put into words the force they bring. Intimidating? Hell yes. But I learned the power of *asking.* The gift of *vulnerability.* And the quiet, unwavering truth that many of them had once been exactly where I was, and they reached back to pull me forward. It was incredible.

Now, don't get me wrong. Not everyone is rooting for you. I learned quickly that some were in it for the power grab, not the partnership. That's where caution comes in. If you've got a gut instinct, *trust it.* If you don't, surround yourself with people who do. Because if you're not careful, you'll get blindsided, flung face-first into the pavement, wondering how the hell it happened. **Be ready. It will.** But so will *she,* the woman who shows up with open arms and armor in the trunk.

Leading a team while still learning to trust my own voice. Selling big visions while fighting small doubts. That's where I found my power. Not because everything was perfectly planned, but because I *kept moving anyway.*

Women often wait for that magical moment that feels like "enough:" enough education, enough experience, enough confidence, clarity, or credentials. The truth is, that moment never comes. You create it. You build the courage as you go. And then one day, someone calls you "CEO" or "founder" or "chief" anything, and you realize: I've been enough the whole time. It's not a feeling, it's a decision.

It wasn't until a couple of years ago that I finally stopped downplaying what I do. For the longest time, when people asked what I did for a living, I'd say, "Oh, I'm just a recruiter."

Seriously. "Just a recruiter?" I was leading a company, building a team, changing lives, yet I wasn't owning it. Why? Because no one was coming to hand me a certificate or pat me on the back. So why the hell wasn't I screaming it from the mountaintops?

I began my career in a world that valued order, control, compliance, and cooperation. Leadership, back then, looked like *doing* more, working longer hours, and fixing more. But then it hit me like a ton of bricks: Great leadership isn't about control. It's about clarity.

To get there, I had to _unlearn_ a few things:

- That burnout was a badge of honor.
- That being liked was more important than being respected.
- That I had to know everything to be taken seriously.
- That a seat at the table meant I couldn't flip the damn thing if needed.

Every time I shed one of those beliefs, I got lighter and Incipio got stronger. I've come to believe this: if you surround yourself with people who are gifted in things you're not, incredible things happen. I've learned to own what I bring to the table, my leadership, my vision, my rockstar moments, *and* to be radically honest about the areas in which I'm not as great. That was the turning point. When I finally made the list of what I *sucked at,* I started seeking out the people who were *exceptional* in those areas. I started conversations, shared my passion, and invited them in. Not just to work *for* me, but to build *with* me. That's when the magic really started to happen.

Here's what I want you to know, whether you're building a business or stepping into the room where decisions get made:

1. **Build what doesn't exist, even if they don't get it yet.**
   They'll catch up. Or they won't. Build it anyway.
2. **Say no faster.**
   To clients who drain you. To roles that shrink you. To anything that makes you question your worth.

3. **Hire for alignment, not just resumes.**
   Skills can be taught. Alignment can't. Trust your gut; here, it's louder than the data sometimes.

4. **Lead with clarity.**
   If your team is confused, your mission is diluted. Get clear, then communicate like it's your job, because it is.

5. **Don't wait to be asked.**
   You're not being overlooked, you're being tested. Step in. Speak up. Lead like you already belong.

6. **You don't have to be ready to be chosen.**
   Opportunity doesn't wait for perfect timing. Be bold before you feel ready.

7. **You're not an imposter. You're just early.**
   Growth feels like discomfort because you're expanding. Lean in.

8. **Leadership is lonely; find your people.**
   You need women who get it. Build a circle that speaks your language and tells you the truth.

9. **Define success for yourself.**
   Money, title, peace, impact. Own *your* metrics.

10. **Rest is a strategy, not a weakness.**
    Your energy is your most valuable asset. Protect it like your business depends on it.

When things were finally picking up momentum, with a strong team in place and clients thriving because of the work our partners were doing, it felt *good*. Companies were learning about Incipio every week. We kicked off the year with the tagline: **"2020 when everything becomes clear."** A partner even had ornaments made up for all of us! And by mid-March? Oh, it became *very* clear.

What happened next wasn't in any version of my 2020 business strategy. It felt like watching this beautiful thing we had built, something gaining traction, interest, and real success, slip through my fingers like sand in an hourglass. I couldn't see the bottom. I couldn't see a way out. We had *just* started turning a profit. I *just* started paying myself consistently. And then, *bam.* Everything stopped.

Clients paused contracts. Work dried up. The partners, the effort, the long nights. . . It felt like it was all unraveling. I'll be honest, I was ready to throw my hands up in pure frustration and say, "Screw it." It felt like the universe was screaming, **"Give up!"**

I might've. If not for those women I mentioned earlier. They snapped me back to reality. Truthfully, it wasn't even *me* who found the strength to keep going. I didn't want to. But they reminded me why I started, who I was, and what I'd already come through.

Clients were calling to cancel. So, I pivoted, a word that will forever be associated with this time in business, that I loathe to this day, and at the same time, I'm grateful that I did. I had to figure out how we could *still* be valuable even if it was different, even if it was smaller, even if it meant completely changing what we did. And we did.

We became experts in all things employee-COVID-related, including HR policy, compliance, and safety protocols, as well as regulations that changed rapidly, sometimes as many as two or three times a day. We haven't even scratched the surface of *personal sacrifice,* but if you're wondering, yes, it made itself known loudly and demanded attention.

It was chaos. For companies. For people. For leaders.

We were being asked to base decisions on yesterday's rules while trying to anticipate tomorrow's reality and somehow land on a resolution that only made sense in *that exact moment.* Because the next day? The game changed again. Somehow, we kept playing.

Here's what I know for sure: growth means moving forward. You don't go back. Not when you've fought this hard for your vision. The journey, the missteps, the pivots, and the deeply personal sacrifices shaped a non-negotiable foundation for what I will and *won't* compromise going forward.

I now choose clarity over chaos. Alignment over appeasement. Purpose over performance. I no longer spend energy convincing people to stay. If someone opts out, they make the choice. That's not loss, that's space. And I've learned space is a gift. Outgrowing someone, something, some version of yourself? That's not abandonment. It's elevation.

So, I've elevated my tribe. I no longer beg people to believe in something in which they don't want to partake. I simply build with the ones who do. These days, I take the advice I wasn't ready for before, the kind I used to brush off or avoid. And I offer advice to the women who are now where I once stood:

- Be relentless in maintaining your boundaries. You'll never regret protecting your peace.
- Don't trade your voice for validation. Speak up, even if your voice shakes.
- *Let people grow with you, but don't drag anyone. (I wish I had taken this advice many years ago. If I had, I honestly can't imagine how much further along I would be than I am today.)*
- Celebrate the quiet wins. That's where real confidence comes from.

You'll know who's in. And you'll know who's out. Let them choose. Just keep choosing *yourself.* I know! I know! This sounds so selfish. I struggled with it. Shouldn't I focus on others? Help them reach their full potential? What I discovered is that they aren't going to do it until they are ready. If you're standing at the edge of a decision right now, wondering whether it's too late, too risky, or too soon, I'll tell you what I wish someone had told me: Do it. Build it. Say yes. Even if it terrifies you. Especially then.

If there's one thing to take away from my chapter in this powerful anthology of women writers, let it be this:

You're not too much. You're not too late. You're not behind. You're exactly where you're supposed to be, standing at the edge of something only *you* can build. You don't need permission. You don't need perfection. And no matter what everyone says, even the people closest to you, remember this: if they're not the ones you trust to speak into your future, their opinions are just noise. There will be people who dislike you and may not even know you; let it go.

Sometimes, judgment is just jealousy dressed up as concern. Let. It. Go.

It's no different than the chorus of opinions you get when you're choosing a college, becoming a mother, or making a bold career move. Everyone has something to say. But only a *few* have earned the right to say it. That's why it's so critical to build a **small, trusted circle** of people who are smarter than you, who tell you the truth, and who want to see you win. The courage it takes to be present and do the thing comes with the conviction that tells you that you were meant for more, to build your why with just enough "crazy" to it that you can figure out the rest.

You already mean business.

So stop shrinking, start leading, and own every damn bit of it.

CHAPTER 2

The Power of Connections

Paula D. Barmore

Real Estate Broker, Speaker, Community Builder

in linkedin.com/in/paula-barmore-a055005

f facebook.com/paula.barmore

instagram.com/paulabarmore/

Paula D. Barmore has been a licensed real estate broker since 1994 and built her career on the values of service, leadership, and connection. She is the former president of the Greater Louisville Association of Realtors, where she helped strengthen professional standards and expand opportunities for agents and clients alike. Deeply committed to her community, Paula serves on the board of Apron Inc., an organization dedicated to supporting independent restaurant workers in times of crisis. She is also an active member of the Pewee Valley Women's Club, continuing a tradition of volunteerism that began with her mother.

In addition, Paula dedicates time and energy to causes close to her heart, including Gilda's Club Kentuckiana and the Colon Cancer Prevention Project. Her advocacy reflects both personal experience and a lifelong belief in the power of community support.

Beyond her professional and volunteer work, Paula treasures her roles as a widow, mom, stepmother, and grandmother. She understands that real success is measured not only in business achievements but in the relationships we build and the lives we touch.

• • •

Y ou've taken a big step. Maybe you have an idea. Maybe you've bought or started a business. Maybe you've stepped into a franchise. Maybe you simply need a little help personally or professionally.

Now comes the most important question: **Who do you know?**

The truth is this: the lifeblood of success—whether in business or in life—is connections. Having others who have walked this path before you, or who can help you navigate challenges, is invaluable. No one succeeds in isolation. So again, I'll ask you: **Who do you know?**

GROWING UP CONNECTED

I grew up in Louisville, Kentucky—a "small big town"—and have lived here all my life. My dad was a general contractor and later a developer. He was the toughest boss I ever worked for. My mom was a nurse and a lifelong volunteer, and she was active in a women's club that I still proudly belong to today.

From them, I learned the one big lesson that still guides me: When you build connections and serve others, it will come back around to you in ways you can't always imagine.

Pewee Valley Women's Club is an amazing group of ladies that I am blessed to still be a member of after 30 years. My mom was also a member, and was president when she passed on in 2002. The fantastic friendships and connections made within this small group of members (less than 30) through the years has been priceless. From being part of an investment group with about 15 of the ladies, to just being a part of the club and involved in their charity fundraisers, I have made so many wonderful and lasting connections. I have assisted in at least ten sales that can be directly attributed to my women's club connections.

In my many years as a member, I have connected others within the group with handymen, investment bankers, insurance, health care professionals, to just name a few.

The value of being a member of any group is getting to know others and first seeing how you can be of help to them.

My dad loved to play golf. He always encouraged me to learn to play as an adult, especially for the friendships and value of potential business done on the golf course. One of the best moments of his life was being able to be a founding member of Valhalla. After my mom passed away, I tried to play golf with my dad as much as possible, as it was a way for us to stay connected, and also an easy way to meet other people.

Thanks to my dad encouraging my obsession with the Derby Festival Hole in One (I have qualified for the finals several times), I found several great clients and friendships that I treasure while out on the fairway. Showing up every year and hitting hundreds of golf balls, trying to qualify to hit one ball for $1,000,000, the people that run this event definitely remember and know me. I met an amazing seller with a great house I listed and sold (on a golf course) due to the multiple years we hit balls together. I always made a point of talking with whomever was on the tee box next to me. I would ask them some questions about golf, or where they liked to play, and mention that, if they ever needed a realtor, or knew anyone else needing an agent, to please call me.

YOUR CIRCLES OF CONNECTION

At first, you might think you don't know anyone who could help you with your business questions or personal challenges. But I believe you do. You just may not have reached out in this way before.

Start by thinking about your **circle of influence**, which includes immediate and extended family, friends, and friends' families.

One of the most important connections I shared with my late husband, Anoosh, relates to real estate in a totally different way. I met Mary through Anoosh over 20 years ago, when she was a partner in a restaurant where he was the executive chef. Anoosh and Mary became dear friends, and through him, I also had the benefit of meeting a new friend. Mary's family became like my second family over many years of friendship. Knowing that two of her daughters lived in a neighborhood where I had a listing coming up, I reached out to Mary to see if she was interested in being in the same neighborhood, which led to a life-changing connection.

Over dinner at Anoosh Bistro, we talked through what selling her Victorian mansion and "rightsizing" would entail. Anoosh then sat down and suggested that we purchase the house together, for the time would come when I would probably be a widow, as he was battling cancer. He really thought it would be perfect for both of us to have each other in a multi-generational living arrangement. My amazing husband's idea of us being the perfect housemates after he passed away resulted in a connection I would never have expected to be so important to me, years ago.

The restaurant circle of connections has been incredible through the years, providing introductions to so many people. Never underestimate giving your card to a person to whom you have just been introduced. How long they may keep that card before calling you varies, especially if you do a good job with following up and keeping them in a database.

I am pleased to have helped at least 20 of our restaurant families and connections buy, sell, and find rentals through the years. Many of these people needed several years to work on their credit to be able to purchase a house. I connected them with professionals in credit counseling, mortgage brokers that were patient and, as a team, we could assist when the time was right.

Now, expand that list by thinking about all the groups of which you've been a part. Some of these include people you went to school with (high school and college), church friends, and fellow association members.

College—a lifetime ago, but it is still impactful, with lasting connections to this day. As I was a young single parent, I attended a local community college, then went to a satellite arm of McKendree, a business school out of Illinois. I made some amazing connections while I achieved my business administration degree. One that stands out to me is Michael B. We stayed in touch through the years, and when he needed real advice, I am grateful that he always thought of me as his agent. Many, many years later, I still get calls from a college connection to help him rightsize again, as he gets ready to buy back his grandmother's home and needs an agent.

FINDING MENTORS

So many seasoned professionals are *thrilled* to be asked about their success: what they would do differently, what they would repeat, what advice they'd give to someone new. You don't need to burn yourself on the stove if someone you trust has already told you it's hot.

Today, it's easier than ever to find mentors. Zoom, FaceTime, and online communities mean you can meet face-to-face with people around the world. Organizations like **SCORE** (a national network of free business mentors) are great places to start.

THE POWER OF CONNECTIONS

Don't forget **trade organizations**. They may require a little legwork, but most allow you to attend meetings before joining. Groups like BNI (Business Networking International), Rotary, or Toastmasters are fertile ground for building professional connections.

TEACHERS, INSTRUCTORS, AND LIFELONG INFLUENCES

Think back to your teachers and instructors. They often shape us in ways we don't fully realize until much later.

Horses have been my passion for over 50 years. My love of riding began when I climbed a fence to pet a neighbor's pony. I joined Pony Club and 4-H and found lifelong friends that I am so grateful for today. Having had the opportunity to help friends find farms, large and small, for their animals and families has been a wonderful result of my passion for riding.

I currently ride with two ladies that I fox hunted with 40+ years ago, Heath and Jackie. We share laughter and tears of joy and sadness, and talk as we ride. The more things change in my life, the more they stay the same.

Horses became a source of peace and joy, but also another opportunity for connection. For a season, I taught therapeutic riding for people with disabilities—stroke survivors, children with cerebral palsy, patients with brain injuries. Each week, I met amazing people and discovered entire networks of therapists, doctors, and families devoted to helping others. That period of my life sparked a lifelong desire to serve.

Later, I volunteered with a crisis and suicide helpline—back before Google made finding resources instant. I learned then just how many people are willing to help, if only you ask. Volunteering, I have met so many different people whose paths would not have otherwise crossed with mine. Having the opportunity to stand next to another, learning a bit more about them and why they are also

SHE KNOWS BEST   23

there, opened my eyes to how we can all help each other. From my time on the crisis line, I kept in touch with several of the people I met. I ended up doing four real estate transactions with one of the people from that time in my life and am still in touch with them today. From the connections made long ago to those made today, I am still helping the kids and grandchildren of the people in my life rightsize.

Volunteering is part of my core value of service to others, and also makes a large contribution to the connections in my life, professionally and personally. I have been able to meet so many amazing people through the years. Prior to 2018, I volunteered to help raise money for Gilda's Club, a national organization whose mission is to make sure no one faces cancer alone, all at no cost. I didn't know at the time how much our family would need them after my late husband's cancer diagnosis in February of that year. I continue to volunteer, making meals and raising funds for Gilda's Club. Being able to connect people with others when they need a personal referral, especially in the worst of times, is an honor and responsibility that I take very seriously.

Teachers played a role in shaping these experiences, too. My first grade teacher, Miss Walker, brought her standard poodle to class every day. He carried her purse in his mouth, which made school magical for me. Years later, I learned she was a champion dog trainer. In my twenties, when someone needed a referral, who did I think of? Miss Walker.

Then there was my fourth-grade teacher, Beth Caldwell, also my 4-H leader. She was the kindest soul. Years later, my late husband, Anoosh, and I catered an event at the Conrad Caldwell House in Old Louisville. To my surprise, it was Ms. Caldwell who opened the door. That connection blossomed into multiple catering opportunities—proof that relationships formed decades earlier can resurface in powerful ways.

College professors and professional instructors, too, often remain important connections. Mr. Charlie Hebel, a respected real estate attorney in Louisville, taught classes at the community college I attended.

One of the most amazing opportunities in real estate is a 1031 Tax Deferred Exchange. Mr Hebel was an expert on this, and I owe a lot of my success to a class he taught early in my career. The ability to refer clients to a trusted attorney who could assist with the complicated process, and to get them to the closing table—along with their favorite realtor—led to multiple deals. Decades later, I still turned to him for advice and referrals.

ESSENTIAL PROFESSIONAL CONNECTIONS

Some professional relationships are absolutely critical to your success. These are the people you want in your corner:

YOUR LAWYER

When legal issues arise—and they will—you need someone you can call. From estate matters to business disputes, lawyers protect you, guide you, and often open doors to new opportunities. In my career, some of my best real estate transactions came through estate attorneys who recommended me.

YOUR BANKER

A good banker is worth their weight in gold. In both good and bad times, you want someone who knows you by name and can offer solutions, advice, and introductions. Being able to connect clients with a banker who can quickly make decisions and offer assistance when I help them find property to purchase is one of the keys to my success with connections. Local bankers especially are deeply connected in their communities and can connect you with other business leaders. That trusted referral from one professional to another is priceless.

YOUR ACCOUNTANT OR FINANCIAL ADVISOR

My dad always said, "The books are the lifeblood of success." If you don't know your numbers, you can't reach your goals. Whether you use QuickBooks or a simple ledger, what matters is discipline. A trusted accountant or CPA will not only help you navigate taxes and IRS "love letters," but can also connect you with other professionals. Through the years, my CPA has referred me to many of her clients who need to rightsize. Having that trusted professional recommend me to someone who is starting to think about moving or investing in real estate has led to some wonderful lifelong repeat clients.

YOUR HAIRDRESSER/MANICURIST

This one might surprise you, but don't underestimate the power of your hairdresser or nail tech. Few people interact with such a wide variety of clients, month after month. The salon chair is a hub of community news, referrals, and opportunities. Do you refer people to your hair or nail person? I am so glad to send people to a great stylist, and know that when my hairdresser hears of a client needing a realtor, she gives them my contact info with confidence that they will be taken care of.

THE ART OF REACHING OUT

So, how do you approach someone you don't know personally?

If you're in the same city, invite them for coffee. Be clear that it's just for 30–45 minutes and with a purpose. Have an agenda. Remember—it's not a date, it's a business conversation.

THE POWER OF CONNECTIONS

Above all, don't make it one-sided. Connections should never be about just *taking*. Always think, *What can I give in return?*

Many years ago, a meeting for coffee I had with Lester Sanders, the first African American president of GLAR and KYR, became the start of a lifelong friendship and mentorship. He encouraged me to step up to run for the board of GLAR, and later to run for president of our association. Having an experienced leader introduce me to others who shared their wisdom and knowledge before I accepted the opportunity to lead our organization of over 4000 agents was pivotal in my career. Lester and I have continued to refer business and contacts to one another professionally and with the various local nonprofits with which we are both involved.

Also, please don't say, "I'd like to pick your brain." It sounds transactional and self-serving. Instead, say something like:

- "I heard from [mutual contact] that you're an expert in ___. I'm starting a business and would love your insight."
- "I admire your work in [area]. Could I buy you a coffee and ask about your journey?"
- "I'm exploring [topic] and would be grateful for your perspective. In return, I'd be glad to connect you with resources or people in my network."

By showing respect for their time and making it mutual, you'll build stronger relationships.

BEYOND THE OBVIOUS CONNECTIONS

There are so many other groups that can provide connections, such as:

- Alumni associations,
- Faith communities,

SHE KNOWS BEST   27

- Volunteer groups,
- Neighborhood organizations,
- Professional associations,
- Sports or hobby clubs, and
- Online mastermind groups.

Anywhere people gather, connections can grow. A casual chat at a volunteer event can lead to gaining a client, mentor, or even lifelong friend.

PRACTICAL EXERCISES

1. **Draw Your Circles:** Put "me" in the center. Around it, add immediate family, extended family, friends, and acquaintances. Next, add professionals, mentors, and community contacts. You'll be amazed at the web you already have.

2. **Reconnect:** Reach out to three people you haven't spoken with in a while. A simple "thinking of you" message can rekindle valuable relationships. I have found that reaching out regularly to my past clients over the last 12 years has given me a wonderful opportunity to reconnect, catch up, and even develop new projects together.

3. **Reach Out New:** Identify two people you'd like to meet this month. Ask a mutual contact for an introduction.

4. **Offer Value First:** Before you ask, think, *What can I give?* A referral, a resource, or even encouragement can go a long way.

5. **Keep a Connection Journal:** Track who you meet, what you talked about, and follow-up actions. Relationships thrive with attention. You could also create a simple database to keep up with business and personal relationships.

WHY CONNECTIONS ARE THE SUPERPOWER

At the end of the day, here's what I know:

- Knowledge matters.
- Skills matter.
- Hard work matters.

But connections? **They amplify your power.**

Connections open doors you didn't know existed. They carry you through storms you thought you couldn't survive. They bring opportunities you couldn't have created on your own.

And perhaps most importantly: they remind you that you don't walk this journey alone.

Because the real magic of connections isn't just what you get from them—it's also what you *give*. Being that connector, that encourager, that person who helps others rise—that is success in its truest form.

Chapter 3

She Closed the Gap— Between Her Ears

Amy Rudy

Sales and Growth Coach, Advisor, Speaker

impactsalessystems.com

linkedin.com/in/amyrudy

Amy Rudy works with entrepreneurs and leaders to shift them from "stuck" to unstoppable, building confidence, changing behaviors, and unlocking lasting growth. She **contracts to a financial result, typically to double sales revenue.** Her mission is simple: help business owners and salespeople sell more and make more money so they can build the business they dreamed of, not just the one they settled for.

As a sales coach, business advisor, and founder of **Impact Sales Systems**, Amy equips business owners and their sales teams to break through mindset barriers, master a proven sales process, and achieve measurable results. She built her career around helping people who are great at fulfilling their deliverables but struggle in sales.

Beyond her coaching practice, Amy is a sought-after speaker and trusted advisor. She proudly serves as a professional advisor for the University of Louisville's Family Business Center and the Metro Manufacturing Alliance of One Southern Indiana, a member of the Prosser Career Education Center Alumni Board, and a trustee of Spalding University, contributing to business growth, leadership development, and education across her community.

• • •

D oes this sound familiar? Liz launched her business from a place of confidence and excellence in her field. *I can do this myself,* she thought. *Call the shots and make a lot more money.*

Liz is a brilliant, creative marketing manager with ten years of experience. She built a plan, fueled her network, and felt confident she could launch her own firm. Out of the gate, Liz had her first paying client. Her second and third came along quickly based on her reputation. Without much overhead, she could keep her rates super-affordable. Three years in, she closed her business and took a full-time job with a client.

Her dream of building a business withered due to strain and financial stress. It wasn't a lack of a plan, talent, or desire. Liz's agency went the way of so many *great-at-the-deliverable-but-stink-at-selling* businesses. Why? Because she could not or, to be more accurate, *would* not execute what she dreaded—sales. She didn't like selling, thought salespeople were icky, and believed marketing would keep getting business. Don't be Liz.

What clobbers us in any role, particularly as leaders and owners, is *mindset.* That loud, unreasonable, nagging, interruptive, hag-like voice gets in the way of achievement.

THE NOISE BETWEEN OUR EARS

I solve growth problems for business owners, leaders, and their sales teams. Typically, when people come to me, they aren't hitting top-line revenue numbers or are overly dependent on a few customers. Extended sales cycles, not getting in front of decision makers, and putting out proposals and pricing just to see those things shared with competitors all lead to shortfalls in revenue, stalls in growth, and overall constriction in value of the business. In my firm, I contract to a result: typically, to double sales production. Why does that matter for this story? The biggest obstacle to achieving those results is the battle between your ears.

You've heard of imposter syndrome and many have experienced it. Imposter syndrome is that self-doubting, sabotaging mindset that causes you to question yourself, your decision-making, and your power. It takes the form of negative self-talk you would never deliver so brutally to others. To really get something to grow with deep roots, it takes nitrous, phosphorus, and potassium. . . that is, manure. Yes, I'm a gardener, too. Let's work through the crapola and build a real toolset for strong, resilient, mental toughness.

GRACE, GROWTH, AND 3:23 A.M.

When I first became a sales coach, that ugly old hag in my head used to make too much noise. I'd give her a name, but she doesn't deserve one.

"Why do you think you can help people learn how to sell? You struggled to grow your own software development business."

"You seriously think people who don't know you very well are going to trust you in their business?"

"What are you going to do when it comes to an industry where you're not familiar?"

Reading the thoughts now, it feels a bit silly. But at the time, these thoughts and doubts were lingering, yet kind enough not to interrupt daily work. These sleep-busting thoughts stuck to waking me up at 3:23 a.m. That was my number. 3-2-3.

"Wake up. Were you sleeping? I didn't think so."

"Are you sure you can make this work? Are you sure you can make enough money to support your family and make real, meaningful changes for people?"

That noise happened a long time ago. I figured it out.

Here is the grace I gave to myself. (I love her, and she loves me!) I can only call it grace because it came to me all at once, seemingly well-formed, calmly, and with the deepest encouragement. I decided:

I'm not the coach I was;
I'm not the coach I'm going to be;
I am learning new things every day.

To be good at this, I just have to be better at it than the person I'm helping. That was it. Solved. That truth quieted the noise. I knew I was creating real, measurable change for others.

When I confirm I have skills and experience of value, a true benefit, I *only* have to be better at it than the person I am coaching. Yes, the word *only* diminishes the statement. This is on purpose: the statement simplifies the weightiness to a single, controllable aspect. My skills versus those of the person I help. Singular and measurable. I am more skilled than someone who doesn't know how to price themselves, grow, scale with their resources, and win deals.

There were deals in the early stages of my career I couldn't close that I close easily today. Deals I chased in the beginning I now know I had no chance to close. I've learned how to best qualify and best close new business. In the early days, the level of complexity of work with a client looked much different than it does to me now. I've always contracted to a result—typically doubling revenue. Now, I effect change in behaviors and mindset and achieve results more quickly.

The complexity of this simple statement starts with who you are, exactly where you are at this moment. *I am.* This statement also recognizes growth from the work you put in and predicts more growth and more gains by doing what you already know. Work; try new things; learn.

This isn't a simple shift. It's a full shift in a belief system. I truly still believe that I am not the coach I was. I am not the coach I am going to be. These prove themselves every day. In fact, over the years, I have had this very conversation with nearly every client at some point in their business when they face self-doubt and struggle.

IT WON'T FIX ITSELF AND IT WON'T STAY FIXED

Mental toughness as an owner or leader will constantly be challenged if you challenge the current state of the business. Stretching for growth, making investments, leading, and managing all create opportunities to second-guess yourself or stall out. While operating from a plan reduces the depth or duration of personal friction, there are important considerations.

. . . .

Failure isn't the enemy. Fear is.

. . . .

You have a lot of roles. I do, too: coach, business owner, board member, wife, mom, bonus mom, friend, sister, gardener, budding chef. . . and about 30 more. In every role, you are allowed to fail. The only requirement? Don't fail the same way twice. You and I are allowed to fall short as owners and leaders—so long as we're not risking catastrophic consequences. The point is, failure doesn't define you. It reflects the learning curve. If you never take off the training wheels, you will never wreck. Growth isn't graceful. It's gritty! Failure in pursuit of growth isn't weakness. It's the ticket price for excellence.

Sometimes I talk to people who say, "I don't like to use the word failure. I prefer to call it opportunity." Avoiding the word *failure* doesn't prevent it. It disarms you. In fact, I'd argue the avoidance gives the idea of failure more power and stifles creativity. Embrace failure as the shortest distance to real, meaningful growth. **Give failure the biggest neck-hug you can and accept the gift of learning.**

Once you are okay with failing in the pursuit of something progressive, look at how learning occurs. There are three aspects to specific skill development. First, I'll provide the technical explanation, then the practical one.

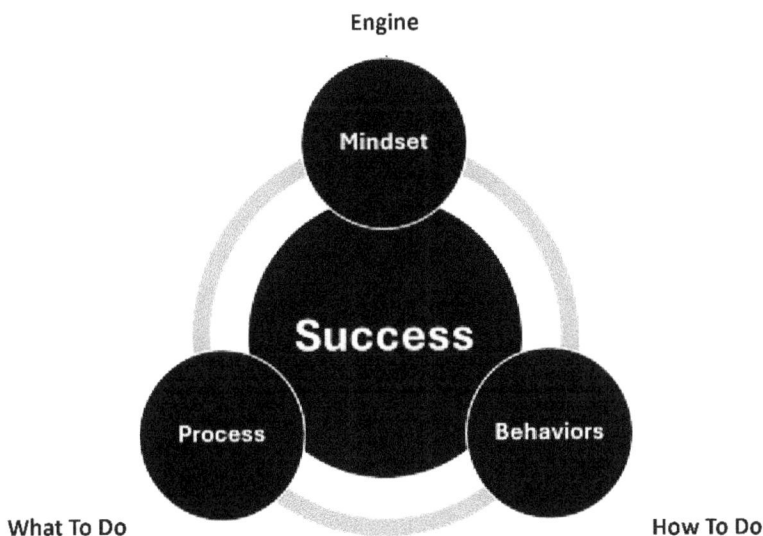

The **process** to the skill you want to learn has steps to follow, technical aspects. This is the easiest to teach and inspect.

Secondly, **behaviors** involve how you perform the skill. This part gets a little trickier; understanding principles or step-by-step instructions only proves you know the process. Performing it is when habits and interpretation create room for mistakes. However, inspection will quickly catch behavioral errors. Retrain and practice.

The *toughest* to observe and correct is the third leg of this triad—**mindset.** It's what goes on between our ears. Mindset is the engine that gives permission or resists. The power of mindset clobbers process and behaviors every time. Mindset is what you believe about yourself, your product, your marketplace, your competition, and even money. What you believe has a stronger foothold than what you know.

My son, Wyatt, became a wrestler and started in kindergarten. He had the process down. Brilliant coaches showed him how to take a kid down with a double-leg takedown. Charge in, pick up the kid, drive him into the ground, crawl up on him, and squeeze until he doesn't move. It's *terrible* for Mom, but he loved it!

But if Wyatt went in at the kid's calves instead of thighs, the other kid would sprawl. Wyatt's face would go into the mat, he'd get two white plugs up his nose, and he would be mouth breathing the rest of the match. (He was the nosebleed king.) If he went in with his head tilted ever-so slightly the wrong way, he would end up in a headlock. At that age, he's not getting out of a headlock.

It's not that he didn't know the right things to do. He knew the process. He did it incorrectly. The behavior failed. Now, what would happen if Wyatt didn't think he was strong enough to pick the kid up? He'd be done before he started.

The same thing happens in leadership: planning a product launch, hiring your first salesperson, managing people, or setting up the strategy of your company. Experts can help fill in the process and provide tools. They can teach and coach on the *how-to-do-it* behaviors. The best coaches and advisors will stick with you through the bumps of mindset fits and starts.

If you're struggling to break through a challenge, take a hard look at yourself. Do you know what to do? Have you practiced, debriefed, recorded, and inspected your performance? Did you leave anything out or create hiding places? Did you demonstrate the behaviors? If you've already proven you know, reteaching isn't the answer.

Start by digging into your mindset. What do you believe about the problem—will it solve itself if you wait it out? What do you believe about yourself—do you trust your ability to handle this? And what fears are in play—fear of failure, fear of success, or fear of being seen trying?

Fear-based mindset barriers are rarely logical. They're emotional, often irrational, and surprisingly persuasive. Once you corner the root of your resistance, removing it takes discipline, courage, and a commitment to act despite the fear. Shifting your mindset isn't about getting more information. You need real reps—low-risk at-bats—to face the fear, expose the lie, and rebuild belief through evidence. Break the emotional hold of fear with logical, compelling reasons why the next step matters—why it's worth doing scared. Then do it. Not perfectly. Not without discomfort. But on purpose. **Your fears don't get to decide for you.**

Once you've fixed your mindset, it might not stay fixed unless you recognize your part in overcoming the barrier. It wasn't luck, and no one else did it for you. You overcame your fear, doubt, and worry. *You* did it. When the wheels get wobbly, remember that you've overcome other obstacles. You've learned through trial and success, and you've learned through trial and error. Keep doing both!

THE CURSE OF "JUST" AND "SHOULD"

"Just" and its friends might seem harmless, but they're confidence-killers. Cut them, especially when you're talking to yourself.

Just is an offensive four-letter word, a curse word.

"I just wanted to see if you'd made a decision on my recommendation."

"I just thought you should know."

"I just need to start working out."

"I just need to do it."

The word "just" is filled with disappointment and regret. It diminishes our efforts, intention, and presence. Unless the intent is to diminish (rarely needed if talking about oneself), statements become stronger without it. Take the first sentence above and remove the *just*. *"I wanted to see if you'd made a decision on my recommendation."* It's stronger, more direct, and asks exactly what you really want to know. It's as if you are trying to take up less space when you unnecessarily include the word "just." Take up your space, sister. You bring value to every space you enter.

I agree there are times when we intentionally diminish things to make them more digestible or to give us courage, such as *"I just have to be better at it than the person I am coaching."* That *just* makes it a truth and builds confidence.

Here's another doozy. "Should-ing" all over yourself. *I should be able to handle this. I should know how to do this. I should be further along. I should. . . Stop.* Do or do not do. Continuing to criticize yourself over things you are not doing is cruel and destructive. If you believe you deserve to be treated better than you treat yourself, the first place to look is the words you plant in yourself.

"Should," when looking forward, is less destructive, but still lacks the commitment and confidence you deserve. *"I should look at expanding our marketing efforts to support growth."* Yes, you should, but will you? Probably not. So, consider changing the thought. *"The right marketing efforts will support growth. I will look at the top three options for expansion of our marketing efforts."*

The offender is the backward-looking "should have:"

"I should have gotten up earlier."

"I should have started working out three months ago."

"I should have replaced that salesperson."

I once spoke with a prospective client about their shortfall in revenue, along with a lack of a strategic growth plan. Their answer, verbatim: *"We should probably start to consider that sometime in the third quarter."* They came off my prospect list immediately.

I'll provide one pass on the use of "should." If the "should-thought" results in forward action, you have my permission, even support, to use "should have."

"I should have considered our staff's reaction to the change in pay structure. The next time I have a change affecting pay or existing policy, I will develop a company-wide announcement to bring managers up to speed as well as one-on-one discussions for employees. That will avoid the confusion I had this time." This "should" is action-driven.

Since you're not allowed to use these on yourself, **no one else is allowed to use them on you either.** Ask for clarification when someone else plops a "just" or "should" on you.

"When you say 'we just have to work harder,' I understand we will have to work harder, but I fully recognize it will be a big lift. Let's talk about how we can do that and where the time might come from. Is that okay with you?"

"I heard you say we should expect to spend 15% more next quarter. Does that mean an increase has been issued and we will spend 15% more next quarter, or is this still in negotiation?"

Words like "just," "should," and the others tend to be hiding places you create for yourself. Watch out for them. What's driving the need for a bailout? Seal off these hiding places and see what happens to your actions, results, and confidence.

IT DOESN'T MAKE SENSE BECAUSE IT CAN'T

Navigating self-doubt, confidence, and ugly old hag noise comes with an extra twist: logic won't defuse it. It won't because it can't. Fear, excitement, worry, and disappointment are all emotions. By their very nature, emotions are illogical and sneaky. That's right. . . psychology enters the fight.

Toni used to struggle to the point of paralysis when it came to picking up the phone to follow up on proposals. Time would pass and her stress would build. She'd sneak an email in from time to time, "just checking in to see. . ." Radio silence. She would eventually give herself the excuse, So *much time has passed, if they wanted it, they would have called back. It's obviously a no.* Mindset stops her from picking up the phone, being persistent in her approach, and utilizing a well-crafted process for these calls. Fear of rejection, embarrassment, and perhaps failure or even success blocks Toni. Not picking up the phone for a direct conversation doesn't make sense, because it can't. It's an emotional choice.

Substitute whatever situation affects you most where you *know* what to do. Where you're struggling to take action, engaging in anything but, and quietly beating yourself up over the thing you are "too chicken" to do.

Why is it so hard? Because it's not logical. I'll let you do the research necessary to take a deep dive into *transactional analysis,* but here's a summary based on Dr. Eric Berne's work. Each of us has three ego states: *parent, adult,* and *child.*

Our **parent** ego state provides protection for our child, having established points of view not based on facts, but on unfounded or outdated beliefs. It is responsible for global, sweeping statements such as, "we don't have money," "you're no good at this," "last time you tried this, you fell on your face," and "no one answers the phone anymore."

The **adult** ego state takes information and determines whether things make sense in justifying a decision or change. For example: picking up the phone logically has a better chance of sparking a conversation to reach a decision than emailing or texting.

The **child** state owns and operates on *emotion*. Your child determines whether they feel safe, things are fair, and how okay or not okay they feel. See all the feelings? There is no logic here. "I don't like making calls." "I don't want to be a pest." "They might get mad at me."

While understanding transactional analysis and how buying decisions are made is crucial in sales (my jam), let's stick to what this means as you battle personal mindset barriers, doubts, and fears.

Using this knowledge to understand the root of doubt and fear provides some muscle and grace in the fight. Understanding whether a child-response is blocking progress is the first step in resolving it. You may notice the use of logic to understand the emotional reasons getting in the way of results and action. Isolating the issues to your child state means you can find a kind, nurturing way to work through the barrier. Critical parents are not welcome here, only nurturing ones. Nurturing parents listen, understand, and encourage action while protecting children. "You can do this. I believe in you. I won't leave you. Go and do it. Nothing bad will happen to you even if you don't like doing it."

It's not that Toni didn't know what to do. Her child ego state didn't feel safe doing it. With coaching, she worked through barriers. She worked on understanding why picking up the phone was important. We practiced the script and what to do if things went sideways. We created low-risk opportunities to make cool outreach calls to help her *child* feel better and know nothing bad would happen.

In fact, something really good happened when she did the work. She won more business because she overcame her mental barrier. She decided emotions were keeping her from doing what was necessary. She worked through understanding the importance of and logical reasons to do the thing. She also confirmed there was no malice or manipulation in her heart when making these calls. She was calling to help the other person. If they reject the offer, her child state understands it's okay. They wouldn't be rejecting *her*. She is safe, albeit uncomfortable. The fact her business desperately needed revenue was not enough of a logical reason to overcome the emotional barrier. Once Toni learned how to recognize and address her child ego state running the show, many things changed. Her confidence increased, others saw her as a stronger leader, revenues increased, and she took incrementally greater chances.

If your inner child is scared, it doesn't matter what your adult ego state knows. She's still not picking up the phone. Recognize her, nurture her, and give her proof she's safe.

YOU ARE NOT TOO NICE.

During the initial meeting with a prospective client, it's not unusual for them to tell me, "I'm not a salesperson." They already have a mindset about what being a salesperson is. And it's not a good one. You must get to the bottom of those barriers and reframe them.

If being a *salesperson* has a negative connotation, dig into what that means. Sometimes it means they had a bad experience with a salesperson. Perhaps they believe that salespeople are gladhanding and manipulative, focused more on themselves than the customer. Well, no one should be *that* salesperson. It's crucial to reframe sales as the role of an advisor who facilitates decisions to root out issues, avoid costs and losses, or fulfill a personal goal or desire. They're someone who has more knowledge and experience than the person seeking help, offering help in a way the person can accept or reject without repercussions. This isn't a one-time conversation, but with work, the barrier can be broken and reconstructed into a strong belief and a highly skilled process. Whether you are in a sales role or a leadership position, early in your career or well-seasoned, **old thinking is baggage.**

While debriefing a sales meeting during a coaching session, Mavis said, "I know, Amy. I'm too nice."

Hold the daggone phone. Mavis and I had a talk. I agreed she is a very nice woman, but what is "too nice?" "Mavis, what do you think I'm asking you to be?"

She was speechless. She recognized giving herself the excuse of being "too nice" to do what her coach is asking meant to "be mean" in some way. First, I would never ask for or encourage meanness, and, secondly, she never would be mean. I shared with Mavis, "You're not too nice. You're *weak* in this skill. It's okay, and we will work on it. But you're not too *nice* to do what is necessary."

Mavis agreed and, as a result, began talking openly about her weaknesses, became more coachable, found comfortable ways to ask questions, and stood up for herself.

You can never be too nice. You can be too weak.

MINDSET ISSUES AREN'T YOURS ALONE

As owners, leaders, and people in sales functions, you are often introducing change or selling ideas.

Mindset, confidence, fear, and doubt show up differently in everyone. No one is exempt from doubt. The question is, does it control your next move?

The core principle of my firm is people don't change because of their problem; they change because of the impact of their problem. Consider the other person's doubts, fears, and resistance when navigating important conversations and facilitating discovery and commitments to change. Their decision-making process will involve their beliefs about themselves, you, change,

> People don't change because of their problem. They change because of the impact of their problem.

exposure, and so much more. Their openness to change begins and ends with an emotional state and is justified logically. Travel on their journey with them.

If you are afraid of asking questions, if you are unsure whether your questions will be off-putting—let them know that before you ask. Ahead of it all, ask permission to have a direct conversation or ask tough questions. **Ask permission. Then be brave.**

FINAL WRAP-UP: WHAT'S IT ALL ABOUT?

Take care of that thing between your ears and she'll take you anywhere you want to go!

CHAPTER 4

Charting Your Career Flight Path: Navigating and Rising Beyond Blocks

Amy Simpson

Human Resources Consultant and Leadership Coach

 www.soarconsultingllc.com

 linkedin.com/in/aesimpson

Amy Simpson brings more than two decades of expertise in human resources, leadership development, and organizational coaching to the table. She earned her bachelor's and master's degrees from Murray State University and held senior HR roles with Best Buy, Zappos, and Discover Financial Services.

Today, Amy is the president and owner of Soar Consulting, LLC, where she partners with small businesses and nonprofits to impart tailored HR solutions and leadership coaching. She is known for her practical yet empathetic approach, equipping leaders with the skills they need to succeed in complex, fast-changing environments.

Deeply committed to community impact, Amy has spent more than ten years supporting the Kentucky YMCA Youth Association and now serves as board chair. She also actively contributes to professional networks, including the International Coaching Federation, Society for Human Resources Management (SHRM), and Louisville Independent Business Association (LIBA).

Amy resides in Louisville, Kentucky with her husband and their three rescue dogs, Cotton, Linus, and Clara.

everal years ago, I was asked if I was interested in a human resources director role with a local nonprofit. It was an amazing opportunity that had the potential to accelerate my career. My immediate response was "no" because I did not think I was ready. I thought I needed more time to learn my current role before moving to the director level. I thought I had to master every qualification before applying. I provided myself some excuse as to why the role was not for me and it was not the right time. Have you ever felt this way? That you were not ready for a new opportunity, or were intimidated by it?

Looking back, I was ready for the role. I could have submitted my resume and gone through the interview process. I could have changed the path of my career. However, I did not have the level of confidence or courage needed to journey down that path. I did not have a **career flight path**.

Almost three quarters of women report that they lack confidence in pursuing career moves beyond their current level of experience. Women only apply for roles when they feel they meet at least 55% of the qualifications. Over 60% of women lack confidence in asking for promotions, and a little more than half lack the confidence to request a new role. You might wonder why this is; that is exactly what this chapter is about. What is blocking women from fulfilling their career flight paths?

When you have a fear, that fear results in blocks that prevent you from moving forward. It also impacts your confidence, due to the fear and other emotions that you feel in those moments. In this chapter, you will lean into understanding your blocks, how to move past them, and how to repeat the process the next time a block gets in your way.

UNDERSTANDING THOSE PESKY BLOCKS

As a certified coach, understanding blocks was a large part of my certification process. They were concepts I knew about in theory, and learned about throughout my career in supporting leaders, but my training provided an opportunity to take a deep dive into truly understanding each block and how to help move clients forward. Understanding blocks and why they keep you from moving forward is the first step in the process.

The four blocks to identify in coaching clients are assumptions, limiting beliefs, interpretations, and inner voices.

Assumptions are thoughts or subjective observations you accept as true without proof or direct evidence. They creep inside to fill gaps in your understanding, often without realizing they are doing so. For instance, you may assume someone is upset with you because they did not respond to your interaction with them in their normal manner. What you may not know is that they just received some difficult news, which has shifted their ability to interact in their normal way. Assumptions create a story in your mind, often without you realizing it, and they shift the story so it doesn't align with fact. Assumptions are tricky little things and often get us into trouble!

Limiting beliefs are deep-seated beliefs that hold you back by shaping how you view yourself, others, and the environment around you. These are usually formed by past experiences and condition our responses. They create fear, restrict growth, and limit your possibility. One of my limiting beliefs is that I am not skilled in the financial aspect of business and therefore should never own my own business or accept a role that has a financial component.

From an early age, I struggled with math. I can remember many long nights when I was growing up, sitting at the kitchen table while my parents helped me make sense of addition, subtraction, multiplication, division, fractions, algebra, and—well, math is *hard*. My limiting belief, "I can't understand math," was deeply rooted.

My ACT score in math was a 14, requiring me to take a remedial math course in college prior to any college level course. Again, this action reinforced this limiting belief to the point I had a tangle of deeply-rooted weeds in my brain on the subject of math. It was going to take a super weed killer to remove them. You will hear how I accomplished this in a bit.

Next are the **interpretations**, which are the meanings or explanations you assign to words, events, or behaviors. Often, these are based on perspectives, experiences, and mindset. I grew up and live in Kentucky, and we are bourbon country. Recently, I spent the day with friends tastetesting bourbon. After each taste, each of us shared a different experience with what we tasted. Each interpretation reflected how our unique senses made sense of the notes in the bourbon.

You and I do this every day when encountering peers, colleagues, family members, and friends. You use your experiences and perspective of the interaction to interpret their words and behavior. When there are changes in the other person's words and behaviors, your interpretations may be false or confused. However, it is difficult to see that in the moment, thus, you interpret this unfamiliar situation based on your perspective, experience, and mindset. Whether that interpretation is true or not may not be something you think about at that moment. Can you think of a time when you interpreted someone's actions incorrectly? How did the incorrect interpretations impact the relationship?

Lastly, I come to the block that talks to you. . . the **inner voice**. The inner voice is ongoing self-talk or internal dialogue that narrates your experiences and thoughts. This inner voice can be supportive and critical. My inner voice, Jamie, has been sitting on my shoulder for *years*. Yes, years. The voice tells me I'm not good at math. She tells me that I can be viewed as too aggressive by male counterparts. She says my ADHD will never allow me to be in control. Jamie questions whether I can be successful. Basically, she uses all the blocks to tell me a false story. The inner voice is sneaky, twisting truths into doubts.

Understanding your blocks is the first step. Using tools to move past them is the heavier lift. Let's dive into how you can move past them.

I UNDERSTAND THE BLOCKS, BUT HOW DO I REMOVE THEM?

Understanding your block and how it impacts your career flight path is the first step to changing the path. Now is the hard work where you must move past your block. **To soar through all of these blocks, there are two tools to use: self-reflection and clarifying questions.** Self-reflection prompts you to take a closer look at the situation. To gain clarity in these moments, ask clarifying questions. Asking yourself "what" and "how" questions can assist in providing clarity to the situation. Let's start with assumptions.

You know what happens when you assume. . . and no one wants that! Being aware of what you are hearing or interpreting is essential when filling in the blanks. Test your assumptions with facts. Be curious with yourself, and wonder what could have happened rather than guessing what happened. For example, "What would cause this person to ignore me when that is not their typical behavior?"

Being transparent with yourself in that you do not have all the facts and then being curious about discovering what may really have happened are key to keeping false assumptions at bay. This prevents you from putting unnecessary blocks in your career flight path.

The limiting belief that I find creeping in to block me is my belief that being weak at math prevents me from moving forward. When I say "I can't" or "I'm not," I limit myself with these beliefs. When do you find limiting beliefs taking over? How do you react when this happens? If you flip the script and ask, "How did I learn this?" or "What about this belief is this still true?" you may find that you can soar past the block.

When starting my own HR consulting and executive coaching business, Soar Consulting, LLC, limiting beliefs showed up like they were the stars of the show! Hello! Here I am! They were calling out, "You will never be successful because you have no idea how to handle the financial aspects of business," and "Do you really think someone is going to hire you to help their company when you can't even balance your own books?"

To soar past this one, I really had to dig deep in self-reflection. I had to consider all the times when my lack of math skills held me back and the times when it did not. I am not a financial whiz, but, over the years, I have learned a few things about P&L statements, managing budgets, and working through compensation plans. In my self-reflection, I found that there were areas where I did succeed in math. In my self-reflection, I also realized that I surrounded myself with people I could lean into when I needed help. I reframed my limiting beliefs into empowering beliefs. I went from the limiting belief of *I can't* to *I can, and when I can't, I know someone who can.* Who really knows everything? Lean into your strengths, and the strengths of others.

Earlier, I mentioned that interpretations are stories that you and I tell ourselves. You simply layer the story over reality. However, what would happen if you built a few alternate endings to your story? How would that help you move past the interpretation into other possibilities? I had a client in this exact scenario.

Carol came to me as a new leader who did not believe she was ready for the role. She had been promoted and started telling herself stories about her interactions with her now direct reports who used to be colleagues. Carol felt that her direct reports did not respect her in this leadership role based on their behaviors. They would stop talking when she came into the room and did not always ask her when they ordered out lunch.

Carol's interpretation was that her leadership was the issue. Carol and I began working through this by first acknowledging that moving from colleague to boss is a tough move for any leader, much less a new one. Then, I started asking what other interpretations Carol could make about her team's shift in behavior. How did the team feel about interacting with Carol in this new role?

Once Carol had alternative stories, she self-reflected on what made these true. She quickly realized that she didn't have many truths, only interpretations. This led Carol to ask how she could have better clarity about the situation. The answer was to engage in transparent communication. Carol decided to have a team meeting and have a candid conversation to better understand their concerns, fears, and excitement about her as the new leader. Carol asked her team, "What do you need in a leader to feel supported and successful?"

She discovered they felt awkward as she moved into the leadership role. This prompted her to ask, "How can I show up to help ease the transition?"

This "how" question prompted a dialogue that provided the clarity Carol needed to strategize her next steps. Those steps were based on real answers, *not* interpretations, creating her career flight path as a new leader.

I mentioned earlier that my inner voice is named Jamie. Naming or labeling your inner voice gives you the power to have a conversation with it. This will likely feel weird, but stay with me. Naming or labeling your inner voice creates distance. It pulls the inner voice out of yourself and puts it into a being of its own. It allows you to challenge the inner voice and flip the script. It prevents the inner voice from overpowering your true voice and strength.

Starting my own business is what I call "scary fun." It was a career flight path that I had thought about but kept telling myself I could never do. All those deep roots of the weeds that "Jamie" had planted told me that I was going to fail and I didn't have the ability to do something of this magnitude. Jamie told me that I was not an entrepreneur. I had only worked for companies and had zero experience in small business.

To a certain extent, Jamie was right. What if I failed? What if my lack of experience would bankrupt me? What if? What if? What if?

There are going to be "what ifs" in everything you do. It is how you answer that makes the difference. Thus, I created the concept of "scary fun" to battle the song of "what if" Jamie kept singing in my ear. It became my mantra when anyone asked me how it was going. I replied, "it is *scary fun!*"

"Scary fun" told me that I would not know if I could do it until I tried. It told me that I had done multiple projects of significant magnitude that were done brilliantly. "Scary fun" told me that I did not have experience in organizational restructures the first time I did one. "Scary fun" told me Jamie was wrong. It told me that it will take courage and confidence to make this work. "Scary fun" also told me that I could write a chapter in a book when Jamie told me to be jealous of other strong women who wrote and spoke about topics. The more I listened to "scary fun's" positive script, the less I listened to Jamie's negative one. I mean, "scary fun" has been more fun than Jamie.

BREAKING BLOCKS WITH CHALLENGE, CONFIDENCE, AND COURAGE

Breaking the cycle of falling prey to your blocks is hard work, and once you have done it, you can and will need to do it again. Like any new adjustment to your behavior, you need to build your tools to repeat the success. The tools that move the blocks from your career flight path are challenge, confidence, and courage.

Breaking Blocks

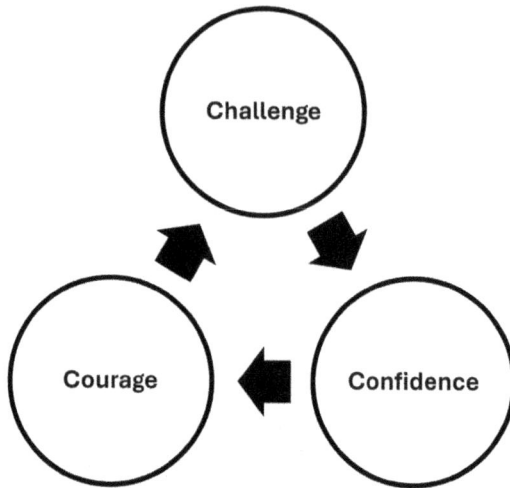

You have to be open to challenging yourself. This purposeful behavior sees blocks not as obstacles but as opportunities to stretch beyond your comfort zone. Challenging yourself reveals where the blocks are hiding so you can address and overcome them. What are your blocks? What is the block trying to teach you? What will you gain if you move past it?

When dealing with assumptions, challenge yourself to be curious and ask hard questions. With limiting beliefs, challenge the belief based on the evidence and then reframe it as an empowering belief. Interpretations require clarity through transparent communication to eliminate the story you are telling yourself. Lastly, your inner voice needs to be challenged and replaced with the positive script you tell yourself. Challenge yourself to turn blocks into growth opportunities for your career flight path.

It is hard to be confident when you do not know if you will succeed. However, is success the *real* confidence builder, or is it the fact you tried? Several years ago, I supported a senior director in a Fortune 300 company as their human resources business partner.

We were challenged by the vice president to improve the employee engagement of all the facilities in his organization. Between the two of us, we built a program that focused on employees helping define the problems about what was not going well in the culture. Through purposeful conversations, groups of employees used this knowledge to build solutions. They were bought into the solution because they were part of the solution.

The program was unlike anything either of us had done. It did not consist of round tables or feedback sessions. It was not a survey or a pizza party to make employees happy. It was an in-depth, six-hour long program that shifted the mindsets of employees to help them feel comfortable working with leadership on issues. I had doubts and fears about whether this new program would deliver the results we needed, but I had confidence in myself that shut down the blocks trying to edge their way into my mind.

The program did work. From a career perspective, it was a "Top Five Career Path" event for me. It was not perfect and needed a few tweaks and changes. It could have failed. It could have been a disaster. I had to have confidence that it could work, just like I must have confidence that I will be successful in my business. Each time you build your confidence, it grows and overtakes those weeds that were previously rooted in your thoughts. You begin to tell yourself that you *can* do this and you *will* make this work. Confidence also provides you a soft landing when you may not succeed by providing you the ability to stand back up when you fail and try again. Confidence looks at your blocks and says, "Not today, blocks. Not today." Confidence is all about building trust in yourself.

Fear, as it appears in our blocks, has a way of hanging out in the back of your thoughts, just waiting for the perfect moment to pop up. Courage cuts through those bursts of fear. Courage is what tells you to take a deep breath and move forward. Courage is hard. Think about courage as the ability to take micro-actions to stretch you just enough to the next step. Courage rewires the message from "I can't" to "I can."

Riding high from the "scary fun" of starting my own business, I committed to my first keynote speaking engagement at my alma mater. This was another one of those bucket list moments for me. I was over the moon, excited and overwhelmed and scared beyond belief. I really thought I had pushed myself too far. Courage pushed me to move forward. I started my speech with a wavering voice. I felt myself trembling and hanging onto the podium. After a few minutes, I found my way, my voice became stronger, and my trembling started to soften. When have you felt really uncomfortable about doing or learning something new and held firm to do it anyway? How did you feel afterwards?

This brings us back to the beginning. Fear is nothing more than blocks trying to keep you from moving forward. They are all mental patterns that shape how you see yourself and the world. Left unchecked, blocks create the obstacles that hold us back from our potential career flight paths. You will not let blocks win because you have the tools to remove them from your path.

The way forward is to use self-reflection and clarifying questions when blocks begin to emerge. From there, challenge, confidence, and courage can help you keep moving forward. Encourage the emergence of new assumptions, limiting beliefs, interpretations, and inner voices because you now have the tools to overcome them, and continue stretching your potential. *You* define *your* career flight path—and it's looking pretty amazing!

Chapter 5

Making an Event Out of Life

Pamela Fulton Broadus & Lauren Broadus

Pamela Fulton Broadus (President & CEO)
& Lauren Broadus (Chief Operations Officer)

splendideventsllc.org

facebook.com/SplendidEventsLLCKY

linkedin.com/in/pamela-fulton-broadus

linkedin.com/in/lauren-broadus

Splendid Events, LLC, founded in 2010 by Pamela Fulton Broadus and her siblings, is a premier event management firm known for transforming visions into unforgettable experiences. Pamela, its owner, president, and CEO, now leads the company alongside her daughter, Lauren Broadus, the chief operations officer. Together, this dynamic mother-daughter team brings creativity, precision, and heart to corporate meetings, conferences, nonprofit fundraisers and private events.

Their work has been featured in many publications and honored with awards, including the Best of Prospect "Best in Event Services" (2015, 2017). In 2020, the firm received the Pivot Award for innovation, while Lauren was named Young Entrepreneur of the Year. Most recently, Splendid Events earned the 2022 Trailblazer Award from the White Rose Wedding Show and the 2024 WBEC-ORV WBE Advocate of the Year Award for Kentucky. Lauren also received the Elgin Award from the Network of Entrepreneurial Women Louisville.

Pam's leadership has been celebrated with the 2014 Salute to Women Entrepreneurs and Emergent Leader Award, the 2016 NAWBO Louisville Epic Award, and the 2022 Louisville Business First Most Admired CEO Award. She has also featured in Who's Who Louisville.

Pamela & Lauren are both members of Alpha Kappa Alpha Sorority, Incorporated and Burnett Avenue Baptist Church in Louisville, KY.

At Splendid Events, LLC, faith, family, and excellence are at the core of everything they do.

● ● ●

"**I**'m thinking of starting a business with my daughter and don't know where to start. Should I lay the groundwork and bring her in later, or should we build it together? Do I need other partners? How will I finance it? Do I need a business plan? How do we merge our personalities? How do we find work-life balance in the event industry?"

If you've ever asked yourself questions like these, you're not alone. They are the same questions that echoed in our own hearts years ago, before Splendid Events, LLC was born. And if you're standing at the edge of entrepreneurship, wondering if you're ready, let us share our story with you.

PAMELA'S STORY

You may be wondering why. Why would I leave a cushy corporate life to venture out on my own? Why would I put everything I had on the line to chase a dream? Why and when did my daughter decide to join me?

The truth is, event planning has always been my dream profession. For thirty years, my career took me into other industries—twenty-five years in healthcare and five in mortgage banking. That journey, though unplanned, laid the foundation for what was to come. I learned the structure, discipline, and leadership that entrepreneurship demands. Despite this, I was restless. Every time I lost a job—2000, 2007, 2009—they called it "downsizing," but I came to see it as God's redirection. Each time, I tried to apply for event planning positions, but no one would hire me. My résumé screamed healthcare and banking.

In 2009, after my final corporate layoff, I felt God say, "I'm giving you what you've been asking for." That was the turning point. Together with my siblings, we launched Splendid Events, LLC on March 25, 2010. We are still standing—stronger, wiser, and more grateful than ever.

But Splendid Events isn't just my story—it's ours. My daughter, Lauren, eventually joined me, bringing her own professional background in education. It turns out, our skills were perfectly aligned. My last corporate role was Director of Product Development, overseeing project managers and ensuring every department was in place to launch a new product. That's exactly what we do in events: make sure every detail aligns before the big day. Lauren's expertise in teaching, organizing, and guiding people added another layer of strength. Together, we discovered that event planning is much like the classroom and boardroom, where every person, every task, and every detail has its role to play.

When people hear that we run a business together as mother and daughter, the first reaction is often, "Wow, I could never work with my mom/daughter!" We laugh because yes, there are challenges, but for us, the gift of building this business side by side has been nothing short of extraordinary!

We like to say that entrepreneurship is not for the weak or the faint of heart. It takes energy, flexibility, organization, resilience, and, yes, thick skin. Mental toughness is a must. But above all, it takes passion. We eat, sleep, and breathe Splendid Events, LLC and we love it.

People often ask us, "How have you successfully made an event out of life?" Our answer is simple. We show up. We prepare with excellence. And then we pour our hearts into the business every day.

Event days are our joy. Whether it's a glittering gala, a nonprofit fundraising walk, a corporate conference, or even something as unique as the Great Bourbon Spelling Bee, we love to see it all come together. The adrenaline kicks in, the room transforms, and we step into our role not just as planners, but as hosts of an experience. We dress up, we run the flow with precision, and we celebrate with our clients as their vision becomes reality. More than once, we've said we must have "the best event team on this side of Heaven," because it truly feels like divine orchestration when everything aligns.

Over the years, we've also been invited to share our expertise with business schools, universities, and community groups. Every time, we return to the same message: building a business is about building a life. Splendid Events, LLC is not just our work, it's our calling.

Looking back, we've realized that this company has made an event out of life itself. Every challenge was a setup for growth. Every setback was a redirect. Every client we've served added to the story. And every event we've designed mirrored the way we've built this business with vision, planning, creativity, and love.

So, if you're standing where we once stood, wondering if you should leap, wondering if you should partner with your daughter, wondering if you have what it takes—our advice is this: start. The answers will come as you walk the journey. The resources will reveal themselves. The balance will be something you create over time.

What matters most is that you say yes to the dream in your heart. Because when you do, you will discover that the life you're building is itself a grand event, one worth celebrating every single day.

LIFE IS THE ULTIMATE EVENT

Every great event begins with a vision, a spark of imagination that says, *"This moment can be more."* For us, that vision didn't just shape weddings, galas, or conferences. It shaped our lives. We've built Splendid Events, LLC on the belief that life itself is the grandest event of all, and every entrepreneur has the power to design theirs with intention, strategy, and joy.

MOMENTS THAT DEFINED US

THE NONPROFIT GALA: MORE THAN JUST A PARTY

Nonprofit events are the heartbeat of Splendid Events, LLC. They are not about glitz, they're about impact. Every gala begins with one question we ask our clients:

"What does success look like for you?"

For nonprofits, success isn't measured by the number of guests but by the **right people in the room**: donors, sponsors, and champions who can advance the mission. That's where we come in.

We help our clients:

- **Choose the right venue,** reflecting the mission, budget, and desired atmosphere.
- **Curate vendors and entertainment,** elevating the event without overshadowing the cause.
- **Design a "run of show,"** seamlessly weaving together storytelling, fundraising, and celebration.

We always say, "We manage the event, so you, the fundraiser, can host the event and raise funds."

That distinction is everything. When nonprofit leaders can focus on relationships rather than logistics, their mission thrives.

BEYOND THE GALA

Over the years, we've expanded far beyond galas:

- **Fundraising Walks and Runs** — We have organized thousands of participants, secured permits, and ensured safety while keeping the mission at the center.
- **Signature Fundraisers** — These include our clients' Great Bourbon Spelling Bee, Brain Ball, and Derby Gala, which combined fun, creativity, and fundraising in one unforgettable evening.
- **Hybrid and Virtual Events** — During the pandemic, we guided nonprofits through mobile bidding, livestreamed auctions, and online donor engagement. Many discovered new audiences and raised more than ever before.

Nonprofit events never just involve logistics. They involve balancing **precision with heart**. We've learned that the right systems allow the mission to shine.

BEHIND THE SCENES LESSONS FOR ENTREPRENEURS

What we've learned from nonprofit events applies to business of every kind:

1. **The Right Room Matters.** Surround yourself with the right supporters. Quality over quantity.
2. **Systems Create Freedom.** A run of show, training, and checklists allows you to focus on what only *you* can do.
3. **Engagement Is Everything.** Keep people connected and involved, whether donors, clients, or customers.
4. **Measure What Matters.** Dollars raised are important, but so are new relationships and visibility. In business, don't just chase vanity metrics.

It's no surprise that, today, the majority of our business comes from nonprofits. They trust us because we understand both **fundraising strategy** and **event execution**—a bridge few can build.

Entrepreneur Takeaway: Ask yourself, what unique bridge do you offer that no one else can? That's your competitive edge.

THE JOY OF EVENT DAYS

After months of planning, event day arrives. The energy is electric. Adrenaline carries us as we dress up, step into the spotlight, and run the event with precision and excellence.

It's the same in business: your launch days, your client presentations, your product releases, these are your "event days." When you've prepared well, they can be exhilarating instead of exhausting.

LAUREN'S STORY

Where my mom brought corporate leadership, I brought operational brilliance.

My background in education gave me a unique gift: I knew how to train. Volunteers, staff, committees—I could take a complex system and teach it clearly. That skill became essential as our events grew in size and sophistication.

I led the charge in:

- **Registration systems** that eliminated bottlenecks.
- **Mobile bidding platforms** that boosted fundraising revenue.
- **Volunteer and staff training** that ensured consistency across every touchpoint.

In today's event world, technology isn't an accessory—it's the backbone. My expertise positioned Splendid Events, LLC as not only creative but also cutting-edge.

Entrepreneur Takeaway: Don't underestimate the power of transferable skills. The thing you think doesn't apply to your new venture may become the secret weapon that sets you apart.

THE CORPORATE CONFERENCE

Corporate conferences are a different kind of challenge: multi-day events with overlapping tracks, trade shows, matchmaking, networking receptions, and meal functions.

At Splendid Events, LLC, we lead regularly scheduled meetings with our clients and their committees. We manage the moving pieces, set the timelines, and ensure accountability. The key is orchestration, keeping dozens of details aligned so that executives, speakers, and attendees can focus on connection and content.

Our transferable skills, project management, systems thinking, and attention to detail are what allow these conferences to flow seamlessly. And we've learned that, in business and in life, clarity and alignment are the foundation of success.

THE REALITIES OF EVENT PLANNING: LESSONS FROM THE FIELD

As event planners, our team members have had the privilege of meeting and working with countless people. The joy of our profession lies in taking someone's dream and bringing it to life, whether that dream is a sparkling fundraising gala, a conference, or a signature celebration. For most of our clients, the process is more than transactional; it's transformational. About 99% of the people we serve eventually feel like family—cheering us on, calling on us again, and staying connected long after the event is over.

But then, there's the other 1%. Those rare encounters remind us that event planning, like any business rooted in service and relationships, can come with challenges. These moments, while uncomfortable, have also been some of my greatest lessons in leadership, communication, and resilience. Let me share two real-world scenarios, as well as how we learned to navigate them with professionalism and grace.

SCENARIO 1: THE DISGRUNTLED COMMITTEE MEMBER

Imagine that you are in the middle of preparing for a major fundraising gala, one you've faithfully managed for five consecutive years. This event benefits a not-for-profit organization, and you're leading a committee of ten people, each responsible for a specific piece of the planning puzzle. Your role is to ensure everything aligns for success.

On this particular day, you gather the committee for a progress meeting. As you greet the group, you notice one member sits in silence. You extend kindness anyway, acknowledging him before diving into the agenda. Halfway through the meeting, the silence breaks, but not in the way you'd hoped. The disgruntled committee member lashes out, voicing his dissatisfaction with the way the event is being planned. His comments aren't constructive, but combative. In a flash, he storms out, pacing up and down the street before leaving entirely.

Hours later, you arrive home only to find his frustration extended in writing. The email reads more like a declaration than a dialogue. He claims he "made a statement" by walking out, questions the event's progress, and accuses you of pushing a "personal agenda." He emphasizes his involvement in several other committees where, unlike this one, he volunteers without issue.

What would you do?

In moments like this, we have learned that professionalism is key. The first step in this instance was to resist reacting emotionally. Even though his words stung, we reminded ourselves that it wasn't about us personally. It was about the event and his perception of it. In the meeting, we knew our best response was to acknowledge his feelings without escalating the conflict. Pamela stated, "Thank you for sharing your perspective. I'd love to set up time with you one-on-one so we can better understand your concerns. For now, let's move forward with today's agenda so the committee can stay on track."

This approach validated his voice but also protected the group's momentum.

When responding to his email, professionalism and diplomacy again mattered most. Rather than matching his tone, we stayed measured. We responded like this:

"Thank you for your feedback. We understand you have concerns about our progress, and we appreciate your commitment to this event. We would like to meet with you individually to discuss your perspective and explore ways we can move forward together. Our shared goal is to ensure the success of this fundraiser and the mission it supports."

He opted to step aside, which was best for the committee and the event overall.

The lesson? Not every committee member will be easy to manage or a good fit, but as planners and leaders, our job is to set the tone. Staying calm, creating space for dialogue, and redirecting focus to the cause are the keys to keeping the event and the team on track.

SCENARIO 2: THE OPPORTUNITY OF A LIFETIME—LOST

Now, let's look at another challenge. Imagine you just wrapped up your second year with a phenomenal nonprofit organization. Together, you've raised half a million dollars to reinvest in the local community. With your help, the organization elevated its gala, incorporating fresh elements, decor vendors, ice sculptures, hotel negotiations, and an unforgettable run of show consisting of a cocktail hour, dinner, live music, auctions, and an after-party.

Their board members and staff sing your praises. The event is a huge success. A few weeks later, you request a debrief meeting. It gets postponed once, twice, even a third time. Finally, months later, you sit down together, expecting to strategize for the future, only to be blindsided with this news:

"We've decided to hire another event planner to replace you."

What would you do?

It's tempting to respond with shock, disappointment, even anger. After all, you poured a year of work into this event. You invested not only your professional expertise but also your heart.

But here's the truth: as painful as it is, rejection in business often has little to do with your performance. Leadership changes, budgets shift, or someone on the board has a personal connection to another planner. Decisions are often political, not personal.

In this moment, grace becomes your power. A professional response might sound like:

"Thank you for the opportunity to serve your organization these past two years. We have truly enjoyed working with your board, staff, and volunteers. We are proud of the impact we created together and wish you continued success with your new event partner. Please know we remain available should you need support in the future."

That's exactly what we did!

This does two things: it protects your reputation and leaves the door open. While you may never work with that client again, others in the room will remember your professionalism. And in the event industry, reputation is everything. This has worked to our advantage time and time again.

FINAL REFLECTION

Event planning is more than logistics and timelines—it's people. The victories are sweeter because of the relationships you build, and the challenges can be spicier because of them, too. Whether managing conflict within a committee or gracefully handling the loss of a major client, the secret is the same: maintain professionalism, protect your peace, and always bring the focus back to the mission.

In the end, even when people are unpredictable, one thing remains constant: the joy of creating moments that matter. That joy will always outweigh the 1%.

So, if you're asking yourself: *Should I lay the groundwork and invite my daughter later? Should I build it with her from day one? How will I finance it? How do we merge our personalities?*

Here's our encouragement: begin where you are. Trust that the skills you've gained along the way, even the ones that seem unrelated, will become the very foundation of your success.

For us, making an event out of life means waking up every day with purpose, living our values, and creating moments of meaning for others.

Your event, your life, is waiting to be designed. Step into it with courage, systems, and heart.

The truth is, the world doesn't need another entrepreneur who simply "does the work." The world needs you: your vision, your passion, your story.

When you embrace that, you'll find yourself not just surviving business, but celebrating life.

CHAPTER 6

Permission Claimed, Not Granted

Jenna Ahern

CEO & Founder

 guardianowldigital.com

 app.guardianowlai.com

 youtube.com/@Guardianowldigital

 open.spotify.com/show/3USzAKcreIZ8tbKvIG8EO6?si=e6616307b9134cbe

Jenna Ahern is the founder and CEO of Guardian Owl Digital, a digital marketing agency, and its AI-powered division, GO AI. She launched GO based on the belief that women don't need to wait for permission to build something meaningful. Under her leadership, the agency has partnered with brands such as Angel's Envy, GE, and the Kentucky Derby Museum, and its campaigns have been recognized in *Forbes*, *Business Insider*, and *Business First*—and earned the Best Data-Driven Campaign honor at the Netty Awards.

A sought-after speaker, Jenna has presented at national events including ESPNW, the National Women in Digital Conference, the National Women in Tech Conference, and at the University of Louisville. She also serves as a part-time AI lecturer at the UofL College of Business and hosts the *GO AI Podcast*.

Guardian Owl Digital delivers a full suite of digital growth solutions from web development and SEO to paid ads, creative production, and AI-powered marketing agents.

Before founding GO, Jenna built her expertise inside three Google Premier Partner agencies and two of the world's largest automotive search engines—Autotrader and Kelley Blue Book. A two-time vice captain of the Division I University of Louisville field hockey team, she brings a competitive spirit and team-first ethos to her ventures.

• • •

W hen I leaped out of corporate America to Guardian Owl Digital, I didn't have venture capital, a high-powered network, or a family business to fall back on. What I had was a sales skillset, laptop, a stubborn streak, and an unshakable belief that women don't need to wait for permission to build something that matters.

It sounds bold when I say it now. At the time, it looked and felt reckless. And maybe it was. I clearly remember my mom saying, "You're crazy, but I believe in you!"

That recklessness evolved into a seven-figure company that's served hundreds of clients nationwide and a team that's as battle-tested as any I've ever been on, and I used to be a Division I athlete!

This chapter isn't about making it look pretty. It's about the messy middle, the hallway of uncertainty, the nights when you question your own judgment, and the mornings when you still choose to show up anyway.

THE SPARK THAT LIT THE FIRE

I spent years in sales and digital marketing at companies like Autotrader and Kelley Blue Book. They were industry giants, and I learned a ton, but I also noticed something: the system wasn't designed for people like me. It was built for people who already had power, connections, or the "right" last name.

I didn't.

What I did have was proof that I could sell, lead, and deliver results. I consistently ranked among the top in national sales, not because I had an easy path, but because my ego at the time refused to be outworked. That drive was ingrained long before business.

As a two-time vice captain on the University of Louisville's field hockey team, I had experienced what it meant to grind. I learned how to lead when you're outnumbered. I experienced what it felt like to play through exhaustion, when your lungs burn and your legs feel like cinder blocks, but you keep pushing because the game isn't over yet. That instinct, to outlast, to hold your breath the longest, not just outperform, became the blueprint for how I built Guardian Owl.

So, when I started, it wasn't to the sound of applause. It was with doubt from others and, some days, from myself.

THE REALITY OF BUILDING WITHOUT PERMISSION

Here's what most headline "entrepreneur stories" leave out: solitude.

When I chose to walk this path, I walked into rooms where people looked past me. They wondered whether I was the assistant. They asked if my husband owned the company. Their words floated above me, but time has a way of revealing what cannot be ignored. I kept showing up. The longer I stood there, the more the energy in the room shifted from dismissal to curiosity.

Being underestimated is not just a trial; it is a teacher. It places a mirror in front of you and asks: will you fracture, or will you forge? I chose to forge.

But endurance alone doesn't keep the lights on, it's just the cost of admission. In the beginning, I said yes to projects that stretched me far beyond what felt safe. Some opened new doors. Others became costly lessons. Yet each carried value.

Every misstep became tuition. Every stumble, a teacher. No MBA could have offered me this curriculum: how to walk without a net, how to trust the ground only as it forms beneath my feet.

> "Every misstep was tuition for the education
> no MBA could give me."

THE GRIND AND THE GRIT

Running a business is often sold like a highlight reel. The truth of it is that it is more grinding than gliding: many of the most valuable lessons arrive through losses.

Clients leave. Contracts dissolve. Balance sheets glare back with more questions than answers. Each moment feels like a test of whether the roots will hold when the storm comes.

One of the fiercest storms came when I realized my cofounder and I no longer shared the same vision. Our "why" no longer aligned, and with every decision, friction deepened.

As the majority owner, I had to make the hardest choice of my career: buying out my partner. On paper, it was a transaction. In life, it was weathering four months of fire while holding only a garden hose. Mornings demanded calm calls with clients. Afternoons pulled me into legal negotiations. Nights ended in silence, staring at the ceiling, wondering if I had just set the forest ablaze.

I remember one night at the kitchen table, papers scattered like fallen leaves, my head in my hands. "Am I crazy for doing this?" I whispered.

Zach looked at me and said, "Trust yourself. I'd bet on you. You'd be crazy not to."

That season taught me that alignment isn't a luxury, it's oxygen. Without it, the tree suffocates, no matter how tall it looks from the outside.

The aftershocks came fast. The very first team member we had hired, someone I had poured into, mentored, and trusted, chose to leave and follow my former partner. The branch snapped without warning, and the crack echoed louder than I expected. I cried. I lost weight from the stress. It felt like a divorce where the children chose sides. I questioned whether I had made myself unlovable as a leader, whether everyone would eventually walk away.

But the broken branch carried its own wisdom: no one owes you anything. People make choices for their reasons, not yours. You cannot cling to them, or you'll miss the chance to grow deeper roots.

Here's the paradox: that loss forced me to rebuild differently. I began hiring not just for skill, but for shared vision and values. Slowly, I assembled a team whose roots intertwined with mine, who didn't just work at Guardian Owl but belonged here. That fracture, painful as it was, made space for a root system for a forest, not just a grand tree.

That's the part of leadership nobody warns you about: when you're the CEO, you don't get to tap out. The team looks to you for vision, even on the days when you don't feel like it. It's your ship and you're sinking or rising with it.

I had to learn how to lead when I felt like breaking. I had to learn how to hold a vision big enough that other people could step inside it, even before it was real.

I had to remind myself, often hourly, that resilience isn't a trait you're born with. It's a mental muscle you build by refusing to give in.

If you're leading a team, this is the moment to ask yourself, where is friction stealing your oxygen? What would you be willing to burn down to protect alignment?

REINVENTION AND RESILIENCE

If entrepreneurship has taught me anything, it's that reinvention is survival.

In the early days, when hustle was my blueprint, Guardian Owl was a scrappy digital agency. Today, we're a seven-figure company that not only manages SEO and digital campaigns but also builds AI-powered marketing agents.

GO AI, our AI agent platform, was born out of necessity. Clients wanted to scale smarter, not just bigger. And frankly, I needed a way to grow the business without burning myself and my team out.

Here's the truth: women are often told to "do more with less." My approach has shifted, literally, to teaching women to do less with more leverage. AI is part of that leverage.

"Leverage beats hustle every time."

The higher lesson? Grinding harder doesn't always move you forward. Sometimes the deeper wisdom is to invest in a system that lets you stop grinding altogether. Reinvention isn't just a strategy; it's the root system that keeps the tree alive when the weather changes.

LEVERAGE VERSUS HUSTLE: A LESSON I LEARNED THE HARD WAY

For years, I wore hustle like a badge of honor because it was the only roadmap I knew. Twelve-hour days, back-to-back client calls, and a laptop that shut only when I did. I thought that if I just worked harder than everyone else, the results would continue to follow. For a few seasons, they did. Hustle got Guardian Owl off the ground. But hustle also nearly buried me under its weight.

The turning point came when a client project almost collapsed because I was spread too thin. I was in the weeds, managing ad copy when I should have been thinking about their bigger growth strategy. That was the wake-up call: hustling harder doesn't scale. Hustle builds walls. Leverage builds ladders.

So, what does leverage actually look like? For me, it took three shifts:

SYSTEMS OVER MEMORY

At first, I was carrying everything in my head: timelines, client notes, campaign goals. Inevitably, things slipped. Once I invested in project management tools and automated reporting, I freed up mental real estate to actually think like a CEO, not a task rabbit.

PEOPLE OVER PROXIMITY

Early on, I hesitated to delegate because I thought no one could do it like me. The truth? Some people could do it better. Hiring experts—writers, analysts, strategists—meant I could stop hovering and start leading. Hustle says, "Do it all yourself." Leverage says, "Build a team that can do more than you ever could alone."

ASSISTANTS OR AI OVER EXHAUSTION

When we launched GO AI, it wasn't about shiny tech. It was about survival. We needed a way to multiply insights and scale smarter without multiplying hours. AI became the wheelbarrow that replaced my two aching hands. Hustle is pouring more sweat into the work. Leverage is building something that sweats for you.

If hustle is sprinting on a treadmill, leverage is building the road that takes you somewhere new.

LEADERSHIP, UNFILTERED

Forget the spotlight. Real leadership happens behind the scenes.

There are days when it feels like you're carrying an invisible weight no one else sees. Decisions that impact your team's paychecks, your clients' trust, and your family's livelihood all fall on you.

Yes, it can feel unfair. But the very loneliness that makes leadership heavy also gives you freedom. You're not here to win a popularity contest. You're here to build.

I learned the essence of that long before I had a C-suite title.

It was the summer of 1996. I was twelve years old, stepping off the bus at my first elite field hockey camp. Everyone else spilled out with gleaming new sticks, crisp hockey kits, and parents who looked like they had just bought half the pro shop. Me? I carried an old, taped-up stick, wearing a t-shirt that was swallowing me, kitted out in gear my mom found in the basement that had seen better days.

My parents had a rule where they didn't purchase new sports equipment for a sport you weren't committed to practicing. I didn't think much of the rule until now.

There were hundreds of girls from all grade schools across the county.

The whispers started before we even hit the field.

"Nice stick!" one girl snickered to another. "That thing belongs in a museum."

I felt my cheeks burn hot and wished I could melt into the grass. I hadn't even taken a shot yet, and, already, I was the underdog.

I had been unaware of how ancient my field hockey stick was and the unorthodox appearance of my shin guards. I literally didn't have the socks to cover the guards. I realized quickly that first impressions do matter, but more importantly, the shape of the stick was so out of date that it was more difficult to control the ball than the newer carbon sticks.

When drills started, the teasing didn't stop. My stick clattered when I trapped the ball, and one girl rolled her eyes loud enough for the whole sideline to feel it. For a twelve-year-old, that moment was devastating. I remember thinking, *Maybe I don't belong here. Maybe they're right.*

Then Coach Linda Kreiser blew the whistle. She walked over, lifted my battered stick in front of the group, and said words that have echoed in my mind ever since: "The talent is in the player, not the stick."

The field went quiet. Suddenly, all the laughter turned into stares—not at my stick, but at me.

Something in me shifted that day. I gripped that old stick tighter, lifted my chin, and decided that it wasn't about winning their approval, but their respect.

By the end of camp, no one cared about my equipment. They cared about the fact that I outworked every drill, outran every sprint, and was a top-notch player. In one scrimmage, I still remember diving for a loose ball, landing flat on my stomach, and popping back up to score. The team members who had mocked me earlier erupted in applause.

That moment taught me that results silence doubt. The labels and judgments people slap on you are nothing compared to what you prove to yourself on the field, in the boardroom, and in life's arenas.

Years later, when I walked into rooms where people assumed I was the assistant instead of the CEO, I thought back to that camp. When clients looked around for a man to deliver "the real pitch," I thought back to that camp. Just like then, I decided to let my work, not their assumptions, do the talking.

Substance beats appearances—every time.

WHAT I WANT EVERY WOMAN TO KNOW

If you're reading this because you're ready to step out of the grind, take on leadership, or build in a space that wasn't designed for you, here's what I've learned:

Permission is overrated. No one's going to hand you the role, the funding, or the title. Stop waiting. Start building. Just *go*. I didn't wait for a green light to leave corporate America—if I had, I'd still be waiting there.

Resilience is your edge. It's not about never falling. It's about standing back up faster than the voice inside that's betting against you. When I lost my first employee to my former partner, I could have let it define me. Instead, I chose to rebuild and rehire with even greater clarity.

Loneliness may be a part of leadership. Don't confuse it with failure. Use it as proof you're in uncharted territory, and that's exactly where leaders belong. Loneliness was the tax I paid for choosing long-term vision over short-term comfort.

Reinvention is survival. When the market changes, when tech evolves, when your gut tells you it's time, pivot boldly. GO AI wasn't a passion project; it was a survival strategy that became an innovation.

Leverage beats hustle. Hard work built the foundation. Smart work sustains it. I've learned to trade twelve-hour hustle days for systems, tools, and people that multiply results.

"Hustle is carrying every brick by hand. Leverage is inventing a wheelbarrow."

THE BIGGER PICTURE

When I think about the past decade, I don't see a straight line. I see a hundred messy zigzags, each one pulling me further away from the safe path and closer to the one I was meant to build.

I even think back to those camp memories and expressing my concerns to my parents about succeeding without a new stick. I recall that my parents sighed and pointed outside to the lawn, where I could go practice and get better using the stick I already had.

That whole week, I remember showing up every day, not knowing anyone, and feeling inferior for not wearing the right brand of socks or even having a "real field hockey stick" at my disposal. I'd stay after and practice in hopes that it would lead to a "purchase" from my dad, but it didn't.

By the final day of camp, I had been running on so much fury I was exhausted of it all. The last day was all games and competitions, where, despite my stick, I actually walked away with a few accolades.

After the final ceremonies, I remember walking to my dad's car and spotting something wrapped in the passenger seat. There was a sticky note on the stick that I wish I still had to this day.

"The talent is in the player, not the stick." – Linda Kreiser

From that moment forward, I was myself on the field and always strived to focus on playing my own game. There is little doubt in my mind that the small gift of mental clarity given by Linda aided in my journey to a full scholarship at the University of Louisville through field hockey.

"The results are in the leadership, not the business."

Don't let the things others say slow you and your goals down. If you let others dictate your truth, you will never be able to center yourself.

Guardian Owl Digital isn't just a business. It's proof that women can start without permission, survive the doubt, and still rise to lead in industries where we were never expected to be, let alone succeed.

GO AI isn't just a product. It's proof that when we embrace change instead of fearing it, we can create tools that position us to live bigger lives, not smaller ones.

My journey? It's proof that resilience, reinvention, and the refusal to wait for permission can carry you further than any connection, title, or funding round ever could. So, if you're on the edge of a decision, wondering whether you're "ready," let me save you the suspense. You're not. None of us ever are. Do it anyway.

Let's GO.

• • •

Conclusion:
The Knowing Woman

When I first started this book, I thought we were collecting stories from women who "made it." What I realized along the way was that we're never really "there." Every one of us, no matter how seasoned, successful, or self-assured, is still learning, still evolving, still becoming.

The women in these pages didn't just tell their stories. They shared their blueprints. They showed what it looks like to rise in the middle of the mess, to lead while still learning, to love what you do even when it's hard. They've shown us that courage doesn't always roar; sometimes it whispers, *keep going.*

If you take nothing else from *She Knows Best*, let it be this:
You are allowed to take up space.
You are allowed to fail, to pivot, to begin again.
You are allowed to want more for your work, your life, your peace.

Because no one's coming to hand you permission. You already have it.

We are a generation of women building without a blueprint, mothers and mentors, founders and friends, builders of businesses and bridges. We are charting new flight paths, redefining leadership, and expanding what's possible for the women who will come after us.

Maybe that's the most powerful legacy of all: when one woman makes use of her knowledge, she creates room for others to rise.

To every woman who picks up this book, thank you for joining us. Thank you for daring to see yourself here. The next chapter of *She Knows Best* isn't on these pages. It's in you.

Now go write it.

Will You Share the Love?

If you've enjoyed *She Knows Best*, the authors have a favor to ask.

Would you consider giving it a rating wherever you bought the book? Online book stores are more likely to promote a book when they feel good about its content, and reader reviews are a great barometer for a book's quality.

Also, if you have found this book valuable and know others who would find it useful, consider buying them a copy as a gift. Special bulk discounts are available if you would like your whole team or organization to benefit from reading this.

Just contact molley@incipioworks.com or
visit https://www.sheknowsbest.net.

• • •

Have an Idea for Your Own Anthology?

If you've enjoyed reading this anthology, imagine the impact of leading your own. Creating an anthology allows you to position yourself as a connector, a leader, and a trusted authority in your field. By inviting your colleagues, clients, or business associates to co-author with you, you give them a powerful platform to share their voice—and you get to shine by association. Everyone benefits from increased visibility, credibility, and the prestige of being a published

author. It's also a smart, strategic way to deepen professional relationships and open the door to new opportunities. Whether your network includes coaches, consultants, entrepreneurs, or experts in any field, an anthology gives them a meaningful way to stand out. If this experience inspired you, consider paying it forward—your own anthology might just be the catalyst someone else needs to take their next big step.

If you would like to explore this, reach out to Cathy Fyock at cathy@cathyfyock.com.

Do You Need a Book Coach?
Let Me Tell You What I Do!

Do you need a cheerleader? I encourage you when you're feeling defeated or that the task is just too hard.

Do you need a brainstorming partner? We work together to discover a new way to approach your topic.

Do you need a developmental reviewer? My clients are often terrified that they will publish a book—a rather permanent bit of documentation—that is less than excellent. I promise you that I will always provide my candid assessment of your work, so you are free to write (and not focus on editing as you write). I read your book as you write it, and again after your rewrites.

Do you need an accountability partner? If you tell me that you need to get this book completed by year end, I will let you know where you need to be to hit that goal at our weekly meetings.

Do you need a visionary? You may have a limited view of your possibilities. I help you think bigger. I encourage you to reach higher. I'm your possibility partner (which was my original tagline when I began my business 10 years ago).

Do you need writing and publishing resources? While I do developmental editing, I don't copy edit, publish, offer legal advice, and other services that you may need. I know great resources that can meet these needs, and I help you select the best resources.

Do you need a teacher to show you the ropes? I offer classes and education on many aspects of writing, publishing, and book promotion, and where I'm not qualified as a teacher, I position other experts to provide educational events.

Do you need a therapist? I now know that I may need to talk you "off the ledge." Sometimes the authorship journey becomes overwhelming, or the negative voices are too loud, and I stand ready to help you get back at your writing desk.

Do you need a trusted advisor? I will tell it to you straight. I have your back. I'm here for you.

I am The Business Book Strategist and I work with thought leaders and professionals who want to write a nonfiction book about their expertise as a strategy to grow their business, their brand, and their business. Since starting my book coaching business in 2014, I've helped more than 250 professionals become published authors.

If you're interested in scheduling a complimentary strategy session, contact Cathy Fyock at cathy@cathyfyock.com.

IGNITE
P R E S S ™

You're an Expert.
Does the World Know It?

Ready to transform your expertise into a bestselling book? Ignite Press is your trusted publishing partner, guiding entrepreneurs, professionals, and speakers to achieve #1 bestseller status and elevate their authority.

Led by international bestselling author Everett O'Keefe, Ignite Press offers personalized consultations covering title development, cover design, book creation strategies, and powerful launch campaigns. With over 150 #1 bestsellers and 33 international #1 titles, their track record speaks volumes.

Whether you're a business leader, medical expert, or thought leader, Ignite Press helps you craft a compelling book that amplifies your brand and message. Better yet, you maintain complete ownership of your intellectual property. You also get your books at cost and receive all royalties.

Take the first step—schedule your free consultation today and discover how Ignite Press can turn your story into a powerful tool for influence and growth.

To learn more, visit https://IgnitePress.us.

www.ingramcontent.com/pod-product-compliance
Lightning Source LLC
Chambersburg PA
CBHW071435210326

41597CB00020B/3801